TRAINS OF DISCOVERY

Operated seasonally as the second section of the *North Coast Limited*, the Depression-era *Yellowstone Comet* offered direct service to Yellowstone National Park, splitting at Billings, Montana, for Cody, Wyoming, and Gardiner Gateway. These happy passengers, departing Chicago in 1930, will spend two days on the train. Author's collection.

TRAINS OF DISCOVERY

Railroads and the Legacy of Our National Parks

Fifth Edition

ALFRED RUNTE

A ROBERTS RINEHART BOOK

Lanham • New York • Boulder • Toronto • Plymouth, UK

Page i: "*North Coast Limited* at Livingston, Montana," original caption and photo-illustration of the Northern Pacific Railway's premier passenger train, from *Wonderland*, 1904. Courtesy of the Pacific Northwest Collection, University of Washington Libraries, Seattle.

Published by Roberts Rinehart Publishers
An imprint of The Rowman & Littlefield Publishing Group, Inc.
4501 Forbes Boulevard, Suite 200, Lanham, Maryland 20706
http://www.rlpgtrade.com

Estover Road, Plymouth PL6 7PY, United Kingdom

Distributed by National Book Network

British Library Cataloguing in Publication Information Available

Library of Congress Cataloging-in-Publication Data
Runte, Alfred, 1947–
    Trains of discovery : railroads and the legacy of our national parks / Alfred Runte. — 5th
        p. cm.
    Includes bibliographical references and index.
    ISBN 978-1-57098-441-9 (hardback : alk. paper) — ISBN 978-1-57098-442-6 (pbk. : alk. paper)
— ISBN 978-1-57098-438-9 (electronic)
    1. Railroads—West (U.S.) 2. National parks and reserves—West (U.S.) I. Title.
TF23.6.R86 2011
385.0978—dc22   2011004559

♾ ™ The paper used in this publication meets the minimum requirements of American National Standard for Information Sciences—Permanence of Paper for Printed Library Materials, ANSI/NISO Z39.48-1992.

Printed in Canada

To my dear friends in the National Park Service, Valley District Interpretation, Yosemite National Park, 1980–1983. Whether you stayed with the parks— or moved on—all of you made a difference. My special thanks to Len McKenzie, Chief of Interpretation, and Vicki Jo Lawson, Valley District Supervisor, for encouraging me to tell this story.

Valley District Interpretation, Yosemite National Park, Summer 1983. Courtesy of the Yosemite National Park Research Library.

✐ CONTENTS ✐

In this poster by Gustav Krollmann (1930), spring has returned to the Paradise Valley of Montana and the slopes of Emigrant Peak, regally positioned to frame the *Yellowstone Comet* southbound for Gardiner Gateway and Yellowstone National Park. Original poster caption, "Absaroka Mountains, Montana, Northern Pacific Railway." 40 × 30 inches. Author's collection.

❦ PREFACE ❦

THIS BOOK BEGAN while I was a seasonal ranger in Yosemite National Park. Then presented as an evening program, it delighted my summer audiences at Curry Village, the Yosemite Lodge amphitheater, and the campground at Lower Pines. Repeatedly, park visitors asked me if there was a book. In 1984, I gathered my slides and commentary into the first edition of *Trains of Discovery: Western Railroads and the National Parks*. In three subsequent, expanded editions, my focus remained on the West. After all, there were no major national parks east of the Mississippi until fifty years after Yellowstone was established. By then the car was a chief competitor with railroads. In the East, the push for national parks came with that difference: railroads had grown cautious about developing parks in the face of the automobile. Obviously, the early railroad monopolies in the West would not be repeated, and even the western lines were having second thoughts about the future of the passenger train.

The purpose of this edition is to complete the story, including a proper overview of the East. For the West, a new chapter details the significance of the 1915 Panama-Pacific International Exposition. The National Park Service, then pending in Congress, could hardly have received a grander boost. In every chapter, there are important new photographs and advertisements, a treasure trove that never seems to end. In chapter 7, I have added several parks to my list of units with special relevance to trains and landscape.

However, even those revisions today would not complete the story. At last, we have come to the issue of land itself. Despite the importance of the national parks, they were never meant as a substitute for open space. The historical mission of American conservation is that greater vision—protecting the landscape we call home.

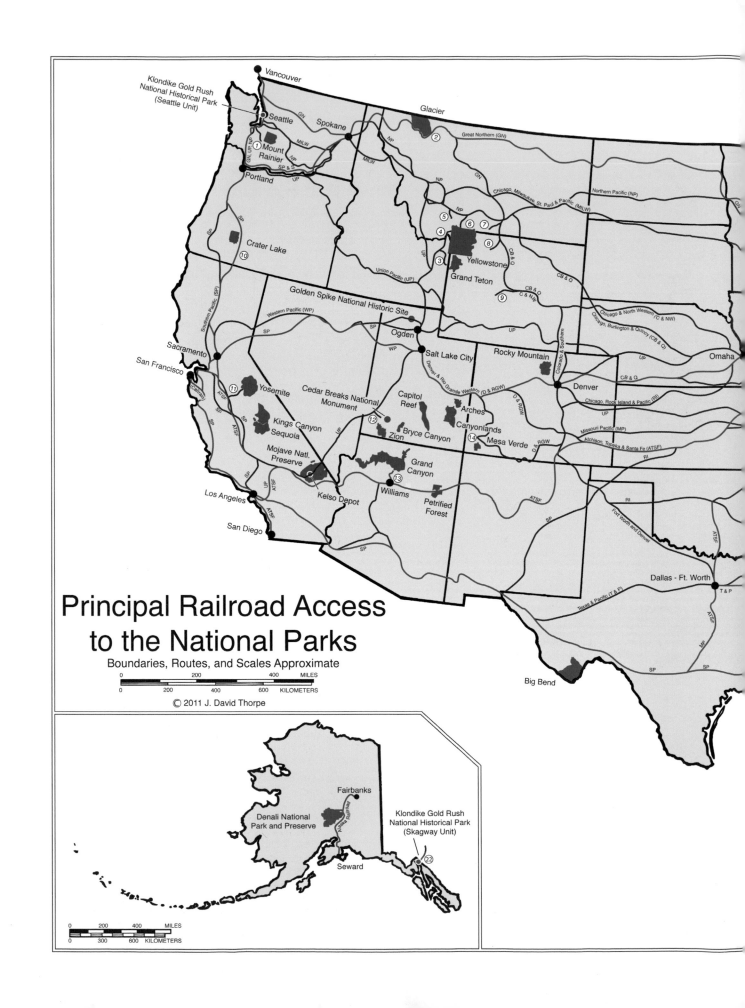

Principal Railroad Access
to the National Parks

Boundaries, Routes, and Scales Approximate

0   200   400   MILES

0   200   400   600   KILOMETERS

© 2011 J. David Thorpe

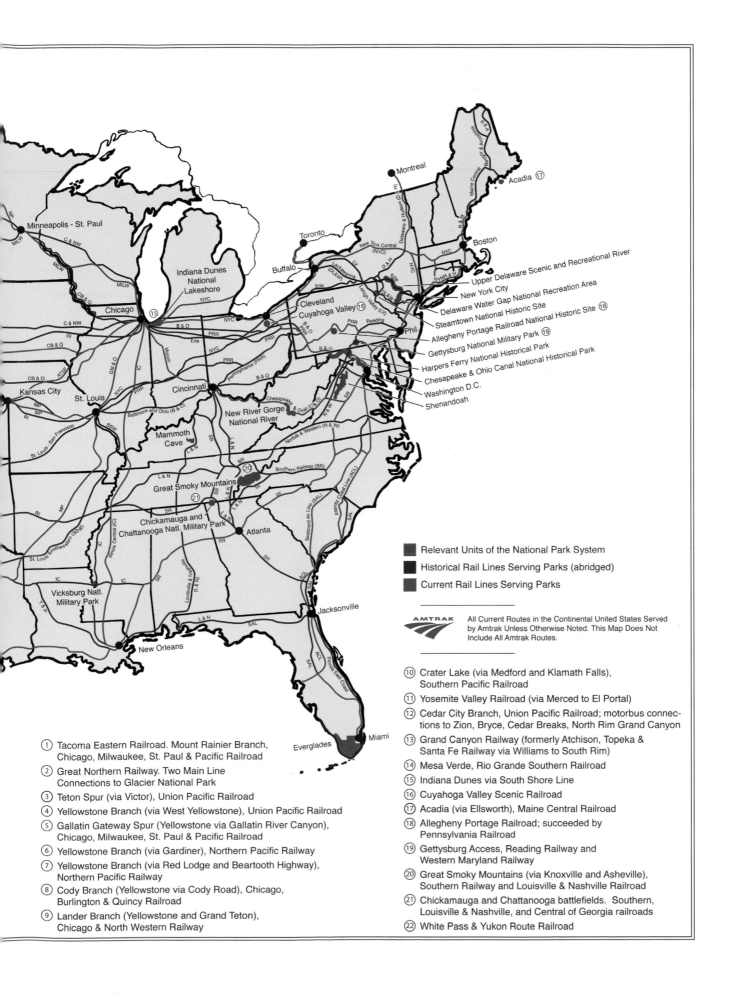

Minneapolis - St. Paul

Toronto

Montreal

Acadia ⑰

Boston

Buffalo

Upper Delaware Scenic and Recreational River

New York City

Delaware Water Gap National Recreation Area

Steamtown National Historic Site

Allegheny Portage Railroad National Historic Site ⑱

Gettysburg National Military Park ⑲

Harpers Ferry National Historical Park

Chesapeake & Ohio Canal National Historical Park

Washington D.C.

Shenandoah

Cleveland

Cuyahoga Valley ⑯

Chicago ⑮

Indiana Dunes National Lakeshore

Phil.

Cincinnati

New River Gorge National River

Kansas City

St. Louis

Mammoth Cave

Vicksburg Natl. Military Park

Great Smoky Mountains ⑳

Chickamauga and Chattanooga Natl. Military Park ㉑

Atlanta

New Orleans

Jacksonville

Everglades

Miami

Relevant Units of the National Park System

Historical Rail Lines Serving Parks (abridged)

Current Rail Lines Serving Parks

AMTRAK   All Current Routes in the Continental United States Served by Amtrak Unless Otherwise Noted. This Map Does Not Include All Amtrak Routes.

① Tacoma Eastern Railroad. Mount Rainier Branch, Chicago, Milwaukee, St. Paul & Pacific Railroad

② Great Northern Railway. Two Main Line Connections to Glacier National Park

③ Teton Spur (via Victor), Union Pacific Railroad

④ Yellowstone Branch (via West Yellowstone), Union Pacific Railroad

⑤ Gallatin Gateway Spur (Yellowstone via Gallatin River Canyon), Chicago, Milwaukee, St. Paul & Pacific Railroad

⑥ Yellowstone Branch (via Gardiner), Northern Pacific Railway

⑦ Yellowstone Branch (via Red Lodge and Beartooth Highway), Northern Pacific Railway

⑧ Cody Branch (Yellowstone via Cody Road), Chicago, Burlington & Quincy Railroad

⑨ Lander Branch (Yellowstone and Grand Teton), Chicago & North Western Railway

⑩ Crater Lake (via Medford and Klamath Falls), Southern Pacific Railroad

⑪ Yosemite Valley Railroad (via Merced to El Portal)

⑫ Cedar City Branch, Union Pacific Railroad; motorbus connections to Zion, Bryce, Cedar Breaks, North Rim Grand Canyon

⑬ Grand Canyon Railway (formerly Atchison, Topeka & Santa Fe Railway via Williams to South Rim)

⑭ Mesa Verde, Rio Grande Southern Railroad

⑮ Indiana Dunes via South Shore Line

⑯ Cuyahoga Valley Scenic Railroad

⑰ Acadia (via Ellsworth), Maine Central Railroad

⑱ Allegheny Portage Railroad; succeeded by Pennsylvania Railroad

⑲ Gettysburg Access, Reading Railway and Western Maryland Railway

⑳ Great Smoky Mountains (via Knoxville and Asheville), Southern Railway and Louisville & Nashville Railroad

㉑ Chickamauga and Chattanooga battlefields. Southern, Louisville & Nashville, and Central of Georgia railroads

㉒ White Pass & Yukon Route Railroad

In the beginning, railroads were among the first to practice what environmentalists today would call restraint. In any comparison between highways and airports, railroads are the most resistant to unplanned change. Highways bring change regardless—shopping centers, subdivisions, strip malls, auto dealerships, billboards, junkyards, and much more. No railroad wished that for the landscape because no railroad could control it. An efficient railroad needs to limit stops; sprawl defies a railroad's need for compact development. Nor was the clutter that became roadside America something the railroads could hope to sell. Even as they opened the national parks to tourism, they were concerned about protecting the scenery along the way. The tourist buying a railroad ticket to a national park was also committing to several days on the train. Every landscape weighed down by unexpected ugliness would only disquiet passengers.

In effect, the railroads were practicing environmentalists a century before the term was popularized. This is also to explain why organized preservationists turned to the railroads in asking Congress for a "Bureau of National Parks." A national parks bureau, the railroads agreed in 1910, was needed to support their own investments in the parks. Those investments had indeed proved substantial, including roads, trails, and hotels. Approved in 1916 as the National Park Service, the agency was exactly what the railroads wanted, promising that the government would finally pay for the infrastructure and allow the railroads to concentrate on attracting passengers.

The sobering realization is how quickly the fortunes of the railroads—and the landscape—changed. In 1929, a daily average of twenty thousand intercity passenger trains operated in the United States. By 1960, the number had fallen to five thousand; in 1970, just four hundred trains survived. On its inauguration in 1971, Amtrak halved those survivors yet again, further insisting that the future of the passenger train was primarily in urban corridors.

Even now, we talk of the money we saved (or think we saved), not the price for landscape. It just had to be (and few in the world agree with us) that the passenger train was "out of date." Granted, we love them in our museums; a few long-distance trains still survive. Otherwise, our country is just too big, we say, to invest in the number of trains we had years ago.

The point is that the moment we accepted the end of the passenger train, we invited a new cynicism about natural beauty. Suddenly, the wonder of distance became an obstacle, something Americans were obliged to "overcome." A growing obsession with destinations replaced our earlier passion for seeing the continent as a rite of passage. In the new American wanderlust, the continent just kept getting in the way.

The final obstacle, many now suggest, is open space itself. A so-called greener world cannot abide unused space; finally, all of our public lands must be put to work.

Our prairies and plains should be supporting wind farms, just as solar plants need our deserts. Nor should any mountain range block America's path toward energy independence. If there is an answer to global warming, it cannot possibly be railroads respecting landscape. America the Beautiful is purely sentiment. What the future needs is a greener car.

Really, is that what we mean by renewable energy—renew our addiction with asphalt and lose the land? What is inspirational about making the land our ultimate throwaway? And yet that is exactly what we are about to do. What is green about forever building roads?

Although the railroad age was never a perfect age, it taught us the difference between preservation and selling out. Guided by railroads and the national parks, citizens wanting beauty and an advanced technology negotiated in good faith about having both. All learned that level of sincerity from a magnificent country, as introduced to them by railroads. People looked out the window and were comforted that technology and the landscape could coexist.

It was the window of a train, after all. What window, then, will we choose? If another window without beauty, what is the point of travel? We have enough windows with cheerless views. When America the Beautiful is gone—the physical beauty—will the pictures of it ever console us? If not, it is time the history in these pages was reinvented. We loved railroads once and must again.

Suggesting the plume of Yellowstone's Old Faithful Geyser, the cover of this Union Pacific brochure (ca. 1955) invites passengers to forsake airline travel for the intimacy of the American land. Author's collection.

Every season brings its own beauty to the Water Level Route

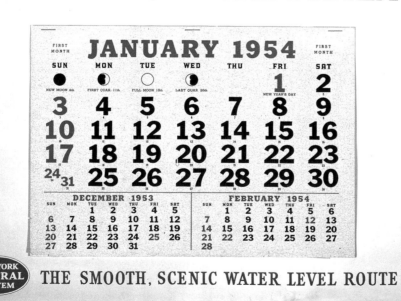

Renowned as the centerpiece of the Hudson River school of art, the Hudson River Valley of New York State attracted railroad artists well into the twentieth century. An intimacy between nature and people remains the theme of this calendar painting by John Gould. Do children today show the same affection for highways? Author's collection.

⚜ ONE ⚜

Nature's Forgotten Allies

Even the soulless Southern Pacific R.R. Co., never counted on for anything good, helped nobly in pushing the bill for [Yosemite] park through Congress.

—John Muir, 1895

Each passing look at nook or brook
Unfolds a flying picture book
Of landscape bright, or mountain height
Beside the Road of Anthracite.

—Lackawanna Railroad advertising jingle, ca. 1910

AS A DEMOCRACY, the United States has been recognized for two achievements—the Declaration of Independence and the national parks. The first, by declaring "that all men are created equal," ensured the advancement of civil rights. The second, by proclaiming the need for preservation, meant that democracy would include the land. Historically, Americans have credited the national park idea to John Muir, members of the Sierra Club, and other like-minded idealists. However, there is another side to the story. America's railroads supported the national parks with a conviction that even the Sierra Club begrudgingly praised. Granted, the railroads were after profits. Yet without the railroads (and certainly no auto company offered like support), Congress was not about to establish national parks just on the conviction of preservationists.

Jasper Francis Cropsey's *Starrucca Viaduct, Pennsylvania* (1865) is a revealing example of the Hudson River school of art. In the middle distance, the train is cradled by a forested mountainside, assuring us that railroads blend with nature. Note that the smoke plume from the locomotive suggests just another low-hanging cloud. Oil on canvas, 22⅜ × 36⅜ inches. Courtesy of the Toledo Museum of Art, Toledo, Ohio. Purchased through the Florence Scott Libbey Bequest in Memory of her Father, Maurice A. Scott.

Our story begins in the East. By the 1820s, a group of artists known as the Hudson River school had turned to celebrating the American landscape. As they reasoned, nature defined the New World just as the rise of civilization defined the Old. No doubt, Europe had marvelous architecture; however, much of its natural world had been lost. In America, the wilderness of creation was still intact. God was everywhere in his natural cathedral, speaking through flowers, trees, clouds, and rocks.

The point of the argument was that the American wilderness had not been settled and destroyed. Even as pioneers swiftly remade the wilderness, artists still found an inviting landscape. Farms and villages were at least close to nature, with wilderness often surviving in the background.

Finally, the visible presence of the railroad obligated artists to accommodate its changes truthfully. How the artist positioned the railroad in the landscape suggested whether the landscape would endure. A railroad in the distance foretold the likelihood of modest changes; tracks in the foreground seemed pessimistic.

The point is that railroads themselves came to agree with artists that the landscape should be upheld. With more tourists wanting to see the country, a pleasant view of its passing farms and villages was the minimum scene the railroads could hope to sell. Thus, as early as 1858, the Baltimore & Ohio Railroad promoted its right-of-way with a special train for artists and photographers. Stops included the junction of the Potomac and Shenandoah Rivers at Harpers Ferry, Virginia (now West Virginia), and the rugged Cheat River Gorge. Following the Civil War, the promotion of the rural landscape grew apace, with the reminder that wilderness, if increasingly rare, was also best reached by train.

The bond between artists and railroads meanwhile grew in the claim that each railroad had the best scenery. All such claims needed to be illustrated in timetables,

Harper's Ferry from Maryland Heights

HARPER'S FERRY WHERE THREE STATES AND TWO RIVERS MEET

283 miles from New York—731 miles to Chicago

We approach Harper's Ferry, one of the most renowned places of historical interest in the United States as well as one of the most picturesque and beautiful. Our train passes through a tunnel cut through the base of Maryland Heights then crosses the Potomac on a steel bridge in a graceful curve that delights the eye, coming to a halt at the station and John Brown's Monument. Here it was that John Brown of Ossawatomie, Kansas, with his "handful of brave but fanatical abolitionist followers," shed the first blood. The monument, a simple shaft, stands upon the spot where his improvised fort stood more than sixty years ago.

Many claim the Civil War had its birth at Harper's Ferry. And during these four years the railway and equipment of the Baltimore & Ohio was a much contested prize. Trains were halted on the Maryland side by the Union Army, and on the Virginia side by

the Confederate, and the passengers were closely scrutinized. The batteries of both armies were lined up on the tops of the different mountains, pouring shot and shell into and across the little village of Harper's Ferry.

To the left is the Shenandoah River, emptying into the Potomac. Across the Shenandoah is the big mountain known as Loudoun Heights, on the Virginia Side.

Back of the town to westward is Bolivar Heights. Beyond the little Catholic church on the hill is Jefferson's Rock, from which a grand scene of mountain, river and valley can be obtained. It was named after Thomas Jefferson, who said the view "was worth a trip across the Atlantic."

The old United States Arsenal, captured by John Brown and his men, of which nothing remains but the foundation, stood just below the present railway track to the right, along the Potomac.

20   21

From 1930, pages 20 and 21 of the railroad guidebook, *Glimpses from the Observation End on the Baltimore & Ohio: America's First Railroad*, extol the beauty and history of Harpers Ferry, West Virginia, today a national historical park. The B & O had actually begun promoting the site in 1858, the year before John Brown's infamous raid on the federal armory. Author's collection.

From a painting by George Inness, this 1857 view of the Delaware Water Gap shows the changing face of a popular eastern landscape. Similar to Cropsey's *Starrucca Viaduct*, the railroad and train are in the distance where they may be depicted as "lost" in the fields and woods. Courtesy of the Library of Congress Prints and Photographs Division.

brochures, and ads. The advantage for landscape was in the building of public affection for scenery, even scenery the railroads did not actually own. With little government land remaining in the East, preservation depended on private discipline. The Hudson River Valley, as a notable example, was strewn with villages, farms, and estates. Another regional favorite, the Delaware Water Gap, became the annual retreat for thousands of visitors from Philadelphia and New York. The point is that it would take another century—in 1965—before Congress itself stepped in to control development by authorizing the Delaware Water Gap National Recreation Area.

During all that time, preservationists had to look elsewhere to protect the gap. Then offering the critical incentive, the Delaware, Lackawanna & Western Railroad publicized its main line through the gap as the shortest route between New York and Buffalo. It was indeed the perfect summer route for tourists, the railroad noted, crossing three mountain chains, six major rivers, and forests cooled by miles of rushing streams. In and near the gap, an economy of boarding houses and fashionable resorts eagerly followed the railroad's lead. Although there was little formal protection of the scenery, the need was both accepted and understood.

As the annual guidebook for the Lackawanna Railroad, *Mountain and Lake Resorts* did much to popularize the Delaware Water Gap and Pocono Mountains. In the issue for 1903, the water gap is also the cover illustration. Brochure 8½ × 6 inches. Author's collection.

Simply, railroads brought leadership to the idea of preservation; commerce and the landscape should coexist. Looking back, our surprise is purely our own. It is we who have forgotten that earlier reciprocity. To be sure, how much the landscape mattered to railroads is ultimately proved by how many decried the spread of billboards. Operating principally between New York and Chicago, the two largest railroads, the Pennsylvania and the New York Central, naturally competed head to head. Since both could promise their passengers speed and comfort, scenery became the differential. Thus the Pennsylvania Railroad competed for passengers by featuring its ascent of the Allegheny Mountains over the spiral of Horseshoe Curve. The New York Central, reprising the Hudson River school of art, similarly promoted the Hudson and Mohawk River Valleys through the picturesque heart of upstate New York.

One of the timeless symbols of American advertising, the fictitious traveler Phoebe Snow debuted in 1900 to publicize the cleanliness of the Lackawanna Railroad. Unlike most railroads, which used soft coal, the Lackawanna fueled its locomotives with hard coal (Pennsylvania anthracite), sparing rearward passengers from excessive soot and cinders. With that reputation secured, the Lackawanna allowed Phoebe more time to enjoy the great outdoors. These postcards were handed out to passengers celebrating the completion of the railroad's modernization in 1915. 3½ × 5½ inches. Author's collection.

Four Hundred Miles of Beauty along the "Phoebe Snow" Way

Lackawanna Railroad

THE LACKAWANNA RAILROAD is not only the shortest route between New York and Buffalo, but it is the route of the most delightful service and the most fascinating scenery.

The mountains at Delaware Water Gap, and the Pocono Plateau are the crowning view of a clean, extraordinarily picturesque journey, which has given the Lackawanna Railroad the name, *"Four Hundred Miles of Beauty."*

Lying direct and high across mountain chains and table-lands, this route means for the traveler, in the warm months of the year, a delightful coolness and dryness of atmosphere impossible on lower levels.

A glance will show
Why Phoebe Snow
Prefers this route
To Buffalo.
And Phoebe's right,
No route has quite
The charm of
    Road of Anthracite.

Left: Before World War I, the Lackawanna often combined Phoebe Snow with the Delaware Water Gap in ads touting the entire railroad as the route of "beauty." 8¼ × 6 inches. Author's collection. *Above:* Revived in 1949 as a modern streamliner, the *Phoebe Snow* offered daylight service through Delaware Water Gap. This publicity photo was taken in 1950. Author's collection.

Whenever possible, great railroad bridges, like major stations, were designed and promoted as works of art. From northeastern Pennsylvania, the examples on these pages are considered legendary, including listings on the National Register of Historic Places. *Above*: Originally painted by Jasper Francis Cropsey (see page 2), the Erie Railroad's Starrucca Viaduct (1848) leapfrogs the town of Lanesboro. This evocative (and exaggerated) interpretation is by Bern Hill—one of sixty-five Hill paintings commissioned by General Motors for its locomotive poster series (1950–1956). Poster 24 × 18 inches. Author's collection.

ERIE LACKAWANNA RAILWAY COMPANY

DINING SERVICE

Dinner Menu

"Erie Lackawanna spectacular 50 year old Tunkhannock Viaduct at Nicholson, Penna. — One of the railroad engineering wonders of the world."

The Friendly Service Route

Less than an hour's drive from Starrucca Viaduct, the Tunkhannock Viaduct (1915)—here gracing a 1968 menu cover—helped smooth the grade of the Lackawanna Railroad between Scranton and Binghamton, New York. Today, the Steamtown National Historic Site in downtown Scranton rounds out an unforgettable historical district, including arguably the two greatest railroad bridges ever commissioned in the service of commerce and beauty. Menu cover 9½ × 6 inches. Author's collection.

Top left: On completion of the Tunkhannock Viaduct at Nicholson in 1915 (2,375 feet, 240 feet high), the Lackawanna Railroad hailed it as the largest concrete railroad bridge in the world. Photo courtesy of the Library of Congress. *Top right*: After 1848, the Erie Railroad's Starrucca Viaduct at Lanesboro (1,040 feet, 100 feet high) was admired as an engineering and aesthetic masterpiece, and was at the time the largest stone viaduct in the United States. Photo courtesy of the Library of Congress. *Upper middle:* The 1908 Scranton Lackawanna Railroad Station (today the Radisson Hotel) was among the grandest buildings of its time. Thirty-six decorative panels done in colored tiles surrounded the Beaux-Arts waiting room, each a popular scene along the railroad. Photo courtesy of the National Park Service. *Lower middle:* Captured in another period photograph, the Delaware Water Gap guided the Lackawanna main line through the named ramparts of Kittatinny Mountain, here Mount Tammany. No landmark was more envied by the Lackawanna's competitors as an inducement for passenger travel. Photo courtesy of the Library of Congress. *Bottom left:* Addressing the competition of the Lackawanna and Erie railroads, this poster stamp by the Lehigh Valley Railroad touts its route as "the Switzerland of America." Although the view is of the coal-mining town of Mauch Chunk (today Jim Thorpe), the Lehigh Valley also applied the term to its mountain-shadowed main line along the Susquehanna River northwest of Wilkes-Barre (U.S. Route 6). In Jim Thorpe, standout attractions include the Asa Packer mansion, built by the founder of the Lehigh Valley Railroad. Author's collection.

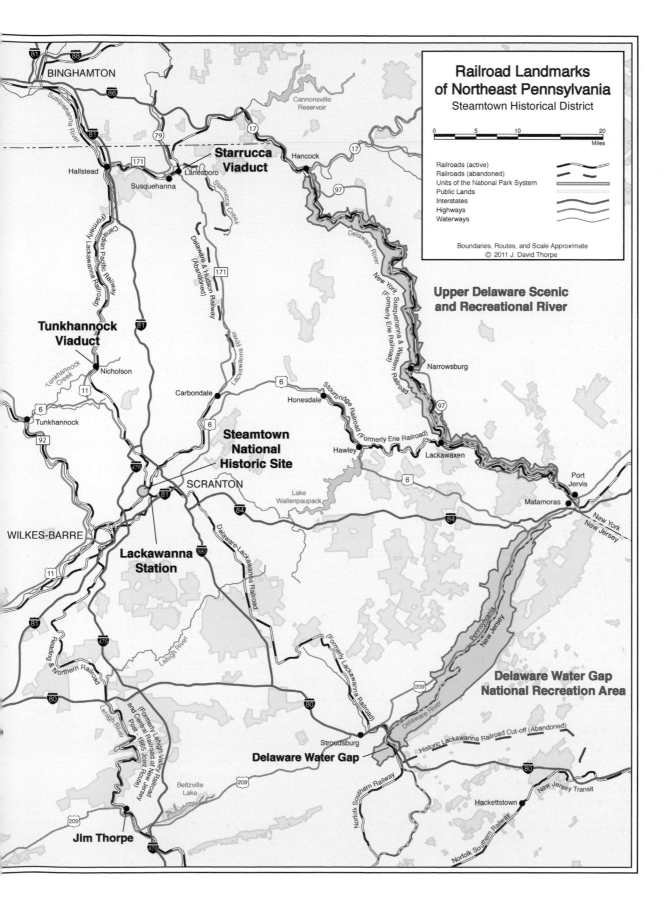

**Railroad Landmarks
of Northeast Pennsylvania**
Steamtown Historical District

0   5   10   20
Miles

Railroads (active)
Railroads (abandoned)
Units of the National Park System
Public Lands
Interstates
Highways
Waterways

Boundaries, Routes, and Scale Approximate
© 2011 J. David Thorpe

BINGHAMTON

Cannonsville
Reservoir

Hancock

Starrucca
Viaduct

Hallstead

Lanesboro

Susquehanna

Upper Delaware Scenic
and Recreational River

Tunkhannock
Viaduct

Nicholson

Narrowsburg

Tunkhannock

Carbondale

Honesdale

Steamtown
National
Historic Site

SCRANTON

Hawley

Lackawaxen

Port
Jervis

Lake
Wallenpaupack

Matamoras

WILKES-BARRE

Lackawanna
Station

New York
New Jersey

Pennsylvania
New Jersey

Delaware Water Gap
National Recreation Area

Historic Lackawanna Railroad Cut-off (Abandoned)

Stroudsburg

Delaware Water Gap

Beltzville
Lake

Hackettstown

New Jersey Transit

Jim Thorpe

The Horseshoe Curve, Altoona, Pennsylvania, by A. P. McDowell, October 12, 1934. Photographic print,

Between them, the Pennsylvania and New York Central shared 10 percent of the nation's total passengers, and therein lay the problem. Advertisers were immediately attracted to those numbers. By ranking billboards beside the tracks—up to several rows deep on level terrain—commercial interests might take prisoner the railroads' passengers, forcing all of them to read the signs. Nor did the "spamming" stop at trackside. Gargantuan signs painted on cliffs facing the right-of-way might overpower it for a mile or more. Opposite the New York Central Railroad, the Palisades of the Hudson River were among the first cliffs to succumb.

Against the argument that advertising was free speech, the railroads sided with preservationists. Ordaining that billboards were ugly and coercive, the railroads ordered their track gangs to tear them down. Advertising blighted the landscape, the railroads agreed, and would not be tolerated on company property. Railroads next extended the restriction to their stations, declaring that waiting rooms, hallways, and entrances should also remain commercial free. "If 'soulless corporations' are thus found willing to set the example of ridding their lines of travel of obnoxious advertisements," wrote a leading journalist, Arthur Reed Kimball, in the November 1898 issue of *The Outlook* magazine, "what may not be hoped from individuals and communities when once the popular aesthetic conscience has been touched?" Meanwhile, between any two railroads traveling "to the same point, one with a line of road placarded with staring signs and the other with a line of road free from such signs, there could be no question of the traveler's choice."

Of course, not every landscape could be protected, whether from billboards or polluting industries. The point is that the railroads thought about billboards—and eradicated them—long before the Highway Beautification Act of 1965. Even while

8 × 46 inches. Courtesy of the Library of Congress Prints and Photographs Division.

conceding the necessities of civilization, the railroads knew what not to change. Factories and mines were necessary, a billboard definitely not.

This is to acknowledge why the public remains fascinated with railroads, even if those memories are today subliminal. A deeper look into any railroad will reveal the tug of landscape. Tourist railroads, dinner trains—even model layouts and garden railways—are incomplete without the scenery. Only a complementary landscape makes them real. We are no less fascinated watching Alfred Hitchcock's movie classic *North by Northwest*. Nor is Cary Grant the only reason. It is the train holding us spellbound, the *Twentieth Century Limited*, winding up the Hudson River Valley. We again miss the reciprocity. Rarely do Americans say of an interstate highway that it has "loved" the land for a hundred miles.

Arriving in the West, the railroads redoubled their reciprocity. In 1898, for example, the Southern Pacific Railroad launched *Sunset* magazine, a monthly periodical specializing in the Southwest and California. Each issue employed dozens of artists and photographers. In 1903, the Atchison, Topeka & Santa Fe Railway similarly began acquiring paintings of the Grand Canyon, Petrified Forest, and other southwestern landmarks for its stations and executive suites. Promoting the Northwest, the Great Northern and Northern Pacific railways likewise commissioned hundreds of paintings and specialty photographs of Yellowstone, Glacier, Crater Lake, and Mount Rainier.

It was the railroads that carried America past its lingering cultural doubts. Writing in 1781, Thomas Jefferson described Harpers Ferry, Virginia, as "worth a voyage across the Atlantic." With the march of railroads across the continent, every American could agree. Although Europe was forever the foundation of Western civilization, the Old World's scenery had been eclipsed.

Above left: Beginning in the 1880s, here from 1889, the Maine Central Railroad promoted Bar Harbor and Mount Desert Island as ideal vacation retreats. In 1919, the rugged beauty of Mount Desert Island inspired Lafayette National Park, renamed Acadia in 1929. 9 × 4 inches folded. *Above right*: An annual publication of the passenger department of the Bangor & Aroostook Railroad, *In the Maine Woods* was rare in promoting wilderness, if with a bias toward hunting and fishing. This cover is from the 1930 edition. 9 × 6 inches. Both author's collection.

From 1929, this colorful brochure by the Maine Central Railroad features Acadia National Park and Bar Harbor, although clearly the railroad is still promoting recreation. 8 × 18 inches open. Author's collection.

It was the national park idea, not a respect for scenery, that came late to the storied East. Preserving landscape, the railroads had done their part, and often for those very places later advanced as national parks. Acadia National Park, Maine, established in 1919 as Lafayette National Park, owed the Maine Central Railroad thirty years of publicity as one of the East's most fashionable seaside resorts. In Virginia, the highland glories of the future Shenandoah National Park (authorized 1926) were similarly promoted by the Baltimore & Ohio, Norfolk & Western, Chesapeake & Ohio, and Southern railways. In the southern Appalachian Mountains of Tennessee and North Carolina, writers and folklorists colorfully referenced "The Land of the Sky." Once again, the Southern Railway adopted and promoted the term years before Great Smoky Mountains National Park (authorized 1926) and the Blue Ridge Parkway (authorized 1933) were established.

A short line railroad served the Hot Springs Reservation, Arkansas, beginning in 1876. The reservation, established in 1832, became a national park in 1921. Other midwestern railroads featured the Mississippi River Valley and the trails of the pioneers. Although slightly off the beaten path, Mammoth Cave National Park, Kentucky, dedicated in 1941, was heavily promoted by the Louisville &

Via Asheville, North Carolina, already a fashionable resort, the Southern Railway promoted the southern Appalachian Mountain region under its popular nickname "The Land of the Sky." The cover of this 1922 brochure is doubly prophetic. Even as the locomotive speeds toward a landscape suggestive of Great Smoky Mountains National Park (authorized 1926), the railroad is losing out to the automobile, whether for recreation or entering wilderness. Courtesy of the University of North Carolina at Asheville, D. H. Ramsey Library, Special Collections.

Nashville Railroad. Appropriately, visitors disembarked its trains at the town of Cave. The railroads also supported the historical parks of the War Department, transferred to the Park Service in 1933. Escalating in the 1890s, aging veterans returned to Civil War battlefields on excursions often organized by the railroads. Those battlefields, too, would become important national parks, if renowned for reasons of a different kind.

Otherwise, the defining difference between east and west remained the availability of public lands. In the West, the abundance of public lands ensured parks the size of Yellowstone, and for railroads a true monopoly. All they need do was be the

In the East, railroad efforts to promote the national parks were generally hamstrung by the lack of formal, railroad gateways. In the West, railroads and parks grew up together. In the East, parks were generally buybacks of private land long after railroad routes had been determined. In this brochure, the Louisville & Nashville Railroad angles for business to Great Smoky Mountains National Park, urging passengers to disembark in Knoxville, Tennessee. 9 × 4 inches folded, ca. 1940. Author's collection.

The authorization of Shenandoah National Park, Virginia, in 1926, prompted this hopeful brochure by the B & O Railroad in 1929. In the not-too-distant future, visitors enjoying panoramic views of the Shenandoah River and Shenandoah Valley would be standing inside the new national park. Meanwhile, this view of the North Fork of the Shenandoah River is actually from Woodstock Tower in the George Washington National Forest. 9 × 4 inches, closed. Author's collection.

GETTYSBURG

ON THE

Philadelphia & Reading Railway

Philadelphia & Reading Railway

Revitalized by the twenty-fifth anniversary of the Civil War, veterans groups spearheaded efforts to preserve its noted battlefields as memorials to the nation's sacrifice. Between 1890 and 1899, four battlefields were thus preserved and placed under the War Department as national military parks: Chickamauga and Chattanooga, Georgia and Tennessee (1890), Shiloh, Tennessee (1894), Gettysburg, Pennsylvania (1895), and Vicksburg, Mississippi (1899). In 1933, all were transferred to the National Park Service. In this brochure, ca. 1920, the Philadelphia & Reading Railway (popularly called the Reading) announces "one day special excursions" to the Gettysburg battlefield from Philadelphia for $2.50 round-trip. Courtesy of Dan Cupper.

Marking the fiftieth anniversary of the Battle of Gettysburg (July 1–3, 1863), more than fifty thousand Union and Confederate veterans descended on the town for what became known as the Great Reunion (July 1–3, 1913). The importance of railroads in making such reunions possible is confirmed in this photograph taken June 30, 1913, noting the veterans' arrival on special trains. Courtesy of the Library of Congress, George Grantham Bain Collection.

first to arrive. By the time eastern parks got under way, the automobile was a serious competitor with every railroad. No eastern railroad was given a chance to build a monopoly comparable to anything found in the West.

In just another thirty years, it was over, all but a skeleton of passenger trains having been cast aside. "I love cars," the columnist Georgie Anne Geyer admitted, addressing the issue in 1977, "but they are simply an amplified version of all the frustrations and confrontations of everyday life. Buses I have never liked. On a train, however, you get, if you look and can see, a deep, abiding sense of the continuity of the processes of nature and life. Pieces fit together. They overlap. People work together. The dependencies and interdependencies of real life are laid out before you like a perfectly woven shawl."

By then, all railroads—even those making room for Amtrak—agreed that freight paid more than scenery. Certainly, freight never complained about missed connections, lost luggage, or delays. On a freight train, dirty windows were never a

In this 1934 brochure, the Chicago, Burlington & Quincy Railroad reassures passengers of its historical commitment to the scenery of the Mississippi River Valley. 9 × 8 inches, open. Author's collection.

problem nor was coffee spilled in someone's lap. Thus chastised by practically every railroad for wanting to take any train, most Americans resigned themselves to taking none. Nor did environmentalists, having turned against industry period, protest as railroads were torn out for bicycle "trails" instead.

For landscape, it meant the end of industrial sponsorship based on a truthful assessment of what was practical and aesthetic. For decades, just the naming of trains after natural landmarks had induced Americans to link the two. Train interiors, designs, and color schemes further celebrated that relationship. A railroad station was a gift of anticipation, and generally the most beautiful building for blocks around. In contrast, the highways paralleling the railroads seemed barren of identity. Ignoring the Highway Beautification Act of 1965, billboards and signs still proliferated. A constant repetition of roadside America—a landscape without aesthetic discipline—conspired to conquer America the Beautiful in ways that no railroad had ever allowed.

The Empire State Express in the Highlands of the Hudson

Beauty-rich and billboard-free, the main line of the New York Central Railroad enters the Hudson River highlands of New York State. The painting is by Leslie Ragan, the official artist for the Budd Company in the 1940s and 1950s. Original period advertisement (detail). Author's collection.

The railroad landscape, Georgie Anne Geyer again reminds us, was something precious and unique. "Cites fade into countryside and rain edges into sunlight and the little houses wait for the whistle that tells them it is all together." As aesthetic disciplinarians, the railroads ensured togetherness from coast to coast. Industrial growth and cities aside, people and the land were never closer. We get no closer just by reinventing labels, now insisting we should be green. Until the landscape is restored to our original honesty—a railroad's honesty—we will never know all that technology offers or in the least what beauty means.

Northern Pacific Station and Gardiner Gateway to Yellowstone Park

From the dining car of the *Yellowstone Comet*, this menu with a painting by Gustav Krollmann alerted passengers to the sights at Gardiner Gateway (ca. 1933). Black and white original, 9¾ × 6½ inches. Author's collection.

❧ TWO ❧

The Northern Pacific Railway

YELLOWSTONE PARK LINE

The traveler who has journeyed eastward to climb the castled crags of Rhineland and survey the mighty peaks and wondrous glaciers of the Alps, who has . . . gazed upon the marvelous creations of Michelangelo and Da Vinci; and stood within the shadow of the pyramids,—may well turn westward to view the greater wonders of his own land. Beyond the Great Lakes, far from the hum of New England factories, far from the busy throngs of Broadway, from the smoke and grime of iron cities, and the dull, prosaic life of many another Eastern town, lies a region which may justly be designated the Wonderland of the World.

—Charles S. Fee, General Passenger Agent, Northern Pacific Railroad, 1885

WHEN AMERICANS think of conservation, they inevitably think first of the national parks. Although conservation comes in many forms, it is the parks that speak to idealism. Accordingly, that America's idealism received a crucial boost from industry may seem almost sacrilegious. Allegedly, the explorers of 1870 originated the national park idea while in the process of opening Yellowstone. The point is that even their altruism had its limits. Yellowstone National Park did not grow in the mind of Congress until the intervention of Jay Cooke, who as the financier of the Northern Pacific Railroad (later to be named the Northern Pacific Railway) hoped to profit from Yellowstone as a great resort.

Simply, legend links Yellowstone to its explorers because their account sounds patriotic. No robber baron aided the national park idea; after all, a national park should be unselfish. America's heroes remain the men of the so-called Washburn Expedition, who, before departing Yellowstone, recapped their findings around what became known as "the Yellowstone Campfire." It was the night of September 19, 1870. Since entering Yellowstone in late August, they had seen the Grand Canyon of the Yellowstone, Yellowstone Lake, and the Upper Geyser Basin. Those wonders were then central to their discussion. Why not simply claim them, the men advised one another? By filing with the government land office for the choicest wonders, every explorer could reap a share of Yellowstone. At that point, Cornelius Hedges, a young lawyer from Helena, Montana, allegedly disagreed. The men should reject any notion of profit, he scolded, and instead promote Yellowstone as a great national park. Nathaniel Pitt Langford, the celebrated publicist of the expedition, then recorded in his diary: "His suggestion met with an instantaneous and favorable response from all—except one—of the members of our party, and each hour since the matter was first broached, our enthusiasm has increased." Thus Langford concluded his entry for September 20, "I lay awake half of last night thinking about it; and if my wakefulness deprived my bed-fellow (Hedges) of any sleep, he has only himself and his disturbing National Park proposition to answer for it."

The nagging question still is accuracy. Langford did not publish his diary until 1905, fully thirty-five years after the event. There probably was a campfire, although not the campfire Langford waited thirty-five years to describe. Embellishments would have been hard to resist, and certainly he edited everything for publication. Nor did the other men around that campfire—half of them also major activists, including Henry Dana Washburn—mention the national park idea in their writings or public speeches during the months that immediately followed.

The missing names are the most telling ones, principally Jay Cooke as promoter of the Northern Pacific Railroad and his office manager, A. B. Nettleton. Indeed, the explorers' campfire discussion that mid-September evening could not have taken place in ignorance of the railroad's plans. Just three months earlier, Cooke had invited Langford to his estate outside Philadelphia. Not only did Cooke retain Langford to promote the railroad, he likely suggested the Washburn Expedition as the means. Langford then carried Cooke's idea back to Washburn, whose position as Montana's surveyor general invited that he be elected to head the party. Throughout, Cooke was the one anticipating the opportunity, namely, that his right-of-way across southern Montana would bring him within fifty miles of Yellowstone. Although runner-up to the Union Pacific Railroad, completed in 1869, the Northern Pacific would be the only transcontinental railroad controlling this grandest of natural treasures. Every prospective traveler (and Yellowstone promised many) would be in the railroad's grip.

Consequently, in part fulfilling his obligations to Jay Cooke, Langford returned east after the expedition to deliver a series of public lectures. Only the Northern Pacific Railroad, he noted, would make Yellowstone "speedily accessible" to tourists. Of course, that is exactly what Cooke had paid him to say.

Meanwhile, the Washburn Expedition had hardly been a systematic exploration, nor had professional scientists been included. That opportunity awaited Ferdinand V. Hayden, a distinguished geologist at the University of Pennsylvania and one of the country's most reputable government surveyors. When Langford's tour brought him to Washington, D.C., Hayden attended his lecture. On the spot, an intrigued Hayden made Yellowstone his priority. Congress agreed and appropriated $40,000, allowing the geologist, as he had hoped, to lead his follow-up expedition during the summer of 1871.

No less aware of that opportunity, Jay Cooke again intervened, this time in a letter from A. B. Nettleton asking whether Thomas Moran might join the group.

The Northern Pacific Railroad's interest in Yellowstone is grandly summarized in Thomas Moran's great painting, *The Grand Canyon of the Yellowstone* (1872). Oil on canvas mounted on aluminum, 84 × 144¼ inches. Courtesy of the National Museum of American Art, Smithsonian Institution. Lent by U.S. Department of the Interior, National Park Service.

Yellowstone's giant geyser, from the pages of *Wonderland*, 1900. Author's collection.

In other words, might Hayden find room for a landscape artist? "Please understand," Nettleton wrote, "that we do not wish to burden you with more people than you can attend to, but I think that Mr. Moran will be a very desirable addition to your expedition." Perhaps a small admission was in order. Naturally, Moran's presence would "be a great accommodation" to Jay Cooke and the interests of the Northern Pacific Railroad. "[Moran], of course, expects to pay his own expenses, and simply wishes to take advantage of your cavalry escort."

Cooke then loaned Moran $500 to make the trip. Better than any lecture or newspaper article, Moran's paintings would bring Yellowstone alive. His field sketches and color studies indeed formed the basis of later efforts to inform the Congress. Moran followed that display in the Capitol rotunda with his masterpiece, *The*

Grand Canyon of the Yellowstone, completed in June 1872. A whopping 7 by 12 feet, it commanded $10,000 from Congress, which hung it in the Senate gallery. Obviously, Moran had no trouble repaying Cooke his loan.

In short, the railroad was still guiding events. As of September 1871, even as the Hayden Survey departed Yellowstone—and despite the comments in Langford's diary—no visible park campaign had emerged. Langford and his colleagues might at least have mentioned their park idea in the wake of the Hayden Survey. Yet no one came forward, not even Hayden, until Jay Cooke made a final intervention.

On October 28, 1871, Hayden received another letter from A. B. Nettleton, asking Hayden to think seriously about a public park:

> Dear Doctor:
> Judge Kelley has made a suggestion which strikes me as being an excellent one, viz: Let Congress pass a bill reserving the Great Geyser Basin as a public park forever—just as it has reserved that far inferior wonder the Yosemite valley and big trees. If you approve this would such a recommendation be appropriate in your official report?

Judge Kelley was Congressman William Darrah Kelley of Philadelphia, a prominent Republican and friend of Cooke's. Like other members of Congress, Kelley had read the report of Lieutenant Gustavus C. Doane, the commander of Washburn's cavalry escort in 1870. Nettleton's reference to "Yosemite valley and the big trees" shrewdly underscored existing precedent. Established by Congress in 1864 as the so-called Yosemite Grant, Yosemite Valley and the Mariposa Grove of giant sequoias were already a public park. The grant awarded jurisdiction to California, provided that the state, honoring the intent of Congress, would hold Yosemite "for public use, resort, and recreation . . . , inalienable for all time." Congress had only hesitated over the issue of management. As a practical matter, because the federal government was in the East (and naturally preoccupied with the Civil War), California likely would prove the better manager. Nettleton's letter now reminded Hayden that Congress might do the same for Yellowstone. If so, it was vital that the territory be withdrawn from entry under the Homestead Act and similar laws. In any case, not until Hayden received Nettleton's letter did he or any of the other explorers—including Nathaniel Langford and Cornelius Hedges—actually lend their services to a park campaign.

Having secured the influence of Ferdinand Hayden, railroad officials stayed out of the limelight. In coming years, most railroad executives would do the same. Always suspicious of corporations, the public might easily misinterpret their advocacy as interference. For achieving Yellowstone, Hayden's fame and reputation should be enough. Indeed, his invited report to Congress did just as the railroad hoped, lending a sense of urgency to the legislation. Claimants had already descended on Yellowstone, Hayden noted, intending "to fence in these rare wonders so as to charge visitors a fee, as is now done at Niagara Falls, for the sight of that which ought to be as free as the air or water." Absent congressional intervention, "decorations more beautiful than human art ever conceived" would be despoiled "beyond recovery." The time for action was now. Jay Cooke and his associates still quietly celebrated when on March 1, 1872, President Ulysses S. Grant signed the Yellowstone park bill into law.

Unfortunately for Cooke, the next several years proved bittersweet. Crushed by the financial collapse of 1873, his personal interests in the Northern Pacific failed. Delayed further by the lingering Depression, the railroad was not completed until 1883. Others then received the honor of opening the spur track south from Livingston, Montana, to the gates of Yellowstone National Park. Regardless, both Cooke and A. B. Nettleton had secured their place in history. Aware that Congress needed prodding, they had made sure it came in time.

Five miles up the mountain past Gardiner Gateway, the palatial National Hotel at Mammoth Hot Springs opened in 1883. The current hotel is a replacement from the 1930s. From *Wonderland*, 1903. Author's collection.

One thing had not changed. Turning finally to the promotion of Yellowstone, the railroad obviously still hoped to build a monopoly, anchored by investors and subcontractors with strong ties to the railroad proper. However, Yellowstone was still a national park. When everyone's zeal got out of hand, the government intervened. The Northern Pacific then quietly made amends through its new passenger agent, Charles S. Fee. Inspired by the supernatural descriptions of Yellowstone, Fee chose Lewis Carroll's popular story *Alice in Wonderland* as the perfect advertising theme: Wonderland! The name further suggested the title for an annual guidebook, beginning with Fee's personal compilation, *Northern Pacific Railroad: The Wonderland Route to the Pacific Coast, 1885*.

Further distancing the railroad from earlier attempts to exploit the park, Fee pledged the Northern Pacific to preservation. "We do not want to see the Falls of the Yellowstone driving the looms of a cotton factory, or the great geysers boiling pork for some gigantic packing-house," he wrote, "but in all the native majesty and grandeur in which they appear to-day, without, as yet, a single trace of that adornment which is desecration, that improvement which is equivalent to ruin, or that

Designed in the rustic style by the Seattle architect Robert C. Reamer, Old Faithful Inn opened in 1904, having cost the Northern Pacific Railway $200,000 in loans to its hotel subsidiary. Of course, the same building in today's dollars would cost many millions. Courtesy of the National Park Service, Yellowstone National Park (photograph 14476).

Although featuring Yellowstone, the *Wonderland* guide-books of the Northern Pacific included many additional articles about western scenery, history, and wildlife. In exchange for six cents to cover postage, the passenger department released up to forty thousand copies annually. On the front cover for 1897, "Liberty" rides an eagle above the Grand Canyon and Lower Falls of the Yellowstone River. In 1899, the eagle has perched on the back cover, now as a symbol for the greater West. Cover sizes 9¼ × 6¾ inches. Both author's collection.

Underscoring the importance of Gardiner, Montana, as Yellowstone's original gateway, President Theodore Roosevelt dedicated the cornerstone of the 50-foot Gateway Arch on April 24, 1903. Accordingly, it is commonly referred to as Roosevelt Arch. Originally intended to pass wagons and stagecoaches, the main opening is 30 feet high and 25 feet wide. From *Wonderland*, 1904. Author's collection.

utilization which means utter destruction." In 1893, the railroad sealed his words with a new logo, the Chinese oval for yin and yang (the balanced universe). A banner curved across the bottom added the proclamation "Yellowstone Park Line."

Next came a restructuring and a name change. Now as the Northern Pacific *Railway*, the line eventually faced serious competition. Arriving at West Yellowstone for the season of 1908, a subsidiary of the Union Pacific Railroad ended the Northern Pacific's twenty-five-year monopoly. In anticipation, the Northern Pacific was already fighting back. From 1883 to 1902, access had centered on Cinnabar, Montana, several miles north of the park. Coordinating with the construction of Old Faithful Inn (1903–1904), the Northern Pacific extended its tracks to a new depot at Gardiner, immediately adjacent to the boundary proper. A fitting companion to

No longer standing, the Northern Pacific station at Gardiner, also by Robert Reamer, gave arriving passengers a foretaste of Old Faithful Inn. Author's collection.

the inn, the Gardiner depot itself combined rustic logs and vaulted ceilings into a magical park preamble. Gateway Arch, dedicated in 1903 by President Theodore Roosevelt, lay just a hundred yards up the hill. From there, it was only five miles by stagecoach to Mammoth Hot Springs, where the National Hotel, an original building from 1883, welcomed arriving guests to the Yellowstone tour.

It would have been surprising had the competition ended there. Five railroads would ultimately serve the park, all following the advice of Frederick Billings. As president of the Northern Pacific in the mid-1880s, Billings cautioned that its entire right-of-way should appeal to passengers, or again, why would people want to come to Yellowstone? In that spirit, all of the Yellowstone River Valley should be protected as the glorious foreground of the national park.

Rarely had a technology more genuinely led to the saving of landscape, if initially because the landscape appealed to tourists. The result was no less effective, whether inside the national parks or out. It remains the distinction of railroads to this day. Although needing the land, railroads rarely gobble it. So it was that a sliver of railroad laid itself across Montana, forever to be remembered as the "Yellowstone Park Line."

Train time at Gardiner Gateway was always hectic. *Top:* In this original Northern Pacific postcard, a stage-coach carries visitors up the hill toward Roosevelt Arch, ca. 1910. *Bottom:* A fleet of park buses boards three hundred college students arriving to take summer jobs in Yellowstone Park hotels, lodges, and camps, ca. 1940. Note the string of waiting buses parked all the way back into town. Both author's collection.

WHERE GUSH THE GEYSERS

OREGON SHORT LINE
ALL RAIL ROUTE TO THE
YELLOWSTONE

With the arrival in 1908 of the Union Pacific Railroad (Oregon Short Line) at West Yellowstone, the competition for passengers grew apace. *Above*: Filled with lavish, color-tinted illustrations, *Where Gush the Geysers* instructed visitors that there was now a second railroad entrance to the park. Cover, 10¼ × 8 inches. Author's collection.

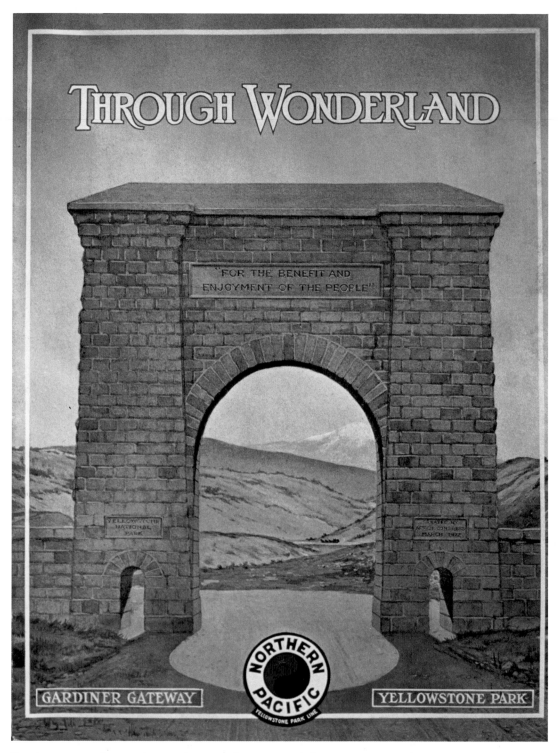

For the season of 1910, the Northern Pacific reasserted the preeminence of Gardiner Gateway with a new guidebook, *Through Wonderland*. Every discriminating visitor should still seek out the arch, Yellowstone's true and original entrance. Inside title page, 10 × 7½ inches. Author's collection.

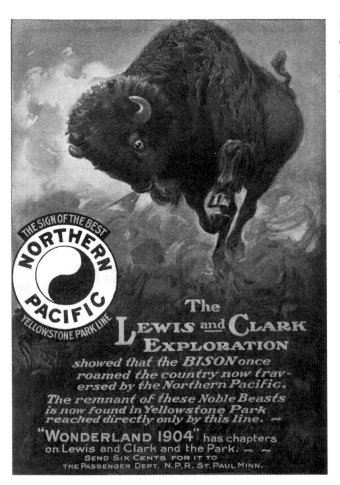

Beyond a tourist destination, public opinion gradually evolved, Yellowstone should also be a haven for native wildlife. In agreement, the Northern Pacific Railway advertised every animal commonly seen by visitors. Of course, fishing was still allowed. All author's collection.

Observing nearly fifty years of railroad service, Yellowstone's timeless emissary, Old Faithful Geyser, majestically erupts in this 1930 poster by the artist Edward Brewer. 40 × 30 inches. Courtesy of Robert Evans.

Encouraged by the Southern Pacific Railroad, early efforts to repeat the success of Yellowstone National Park focused on the High Sierra of California, as reflected in this poster from 1933 depicting the giant sequoias. Part of a major series for the railroad by the artist Maurice Logan, each poster featured a distinctive California or western setting, with special emphasis on the national parks. Here Logan reprises a thirty-year-old photograph of the U.S. Cavalry passing through the Wawona Tunnel Tree in Yosemite's Mariposa Redwood Grove. Printer's proof, 8½ × 6 inches, of printed poster 23 × 16 inches. Proof in author's collection.

☙ THREE ❧

Everywhere West

War with Switzerland! Uncle Sam Fires the First Gun in the New Battle for the Possession of the American Tourist—Mobilizing a Regiment of the Deepest Canyons, the Highest Waterfalls, the Oldest, Largest Trees in the World— Scenery as a New National Resource. . . . Good rail connections to and from the [national] parks, good transportation facilities in the parks, and good hotels and sleeping accommodations are absolutely essential if this government would snare the tourist and divert his steady flow of golden coin from its present course to Europe back into this country.

—Mark Daniels, U.S. Department of the Interior, July 1915

ESTABLISHED IN 1872, Yellowstone would not see its equivalent until 1890. It remained for the rising competition among the transcontinental railroads to give the national park idea a crucial boost. Why stop with Yellowstone? the railroads asked. A great national park should encircle Yosemite Valley and another protect the giant sequoias. In Washington State, tourists were discovering Mount Rainier. Oregon's Crater Lake was known to be an incredible blue. Arizona Territory had the Grand Canyon—a wonder nearly three hundred river miles in length. The Rocky Mountains in northern Montana boasted glaciated peaks and walled-in lakes. Preservationists and the railroads were unanimous. All of those places should be made into national parks.

After Yellowstone, the focus was on California and plans to extend the Yosemite Grant into the high country. The Southern Pacific Railroad quietly agreed. As a practical matter, railroad land grants in the San Joaquin Valley were at risk of flooding if Yosemite were deforested or overgrazed. Farther south, ancient groves of giant sequoias lay sprinkled across miles of watersheds, each also critical to the lands below. Again, the practical supported the aesthetic—and vice versa. On September 25, 1890, Congress and the president approved Sequoia National Park. A subsequent bill, signed October 1, enlarged Sequoia and approved two other parks—General Grant and Yosemite, the latter a whopping 1,542 square miles surrounding the valley proper.

Virtually overnight, a national park *system* had been created. For spearheading the campaign in print, the nation could thank the partnership of John Muir and Robert Underwood Johnson, then associate editor of Century Magazine. The key figure behind the scenes was a public unknown—Daniel K. Zumwalt of the Southern Pacific Railroad. As its land agent in the San Joaquin Valley, Zumwalt spent a month in Washington, D.C., lobbying individual senators and key representatives. Save those critical watersheds, he continued to plead. It was indeed Zumwalt who convinced Congress to enlarge both Sequoia and Yosemite parks, alone more than doubling the size of Sequoia in the bill of October 1.

The nation's fifth national park, Mount Rainier, restored the preeminence of the Northern Pacific Railway, although this time with a blatantly commercial twist. As authorized by its land grant to the Pacific, the Northern Pacific controlled half the mountain in alternating square mile blocks. The government sections remained in public ownership. Nothing could seriously distract from the glories of Mount Rainier, the railroad realized. Tourism would always be secure. Meanwhile, the railroad saw little of commercial value in its checkerboard blocks of ice and snow.

A national park bill offered the perfect opportunity to exchange those holdings for better lands well removed from the peak. The railroad asked for an even trade—and got it, receiving, acre for acre, lowland timber worth so much more. Congress then sealed the railroad's wishes—and the park—in the enabling act of February 1899.

As a major corporate windfall (the timber gained was incredibly rich), the incident would later remind historians that the railroads could be devious even when doing good. The point is that the traveling public remembered the good—the beauty that was freed of conflict. Timbered lands were commonplace and national parks still few.

A regional railroad, the Tacoma Eastern, next looked forward to exploiting both. Charted in 1890, its construction was halted by the Depression of 1893. When construction resumed at the turn of the century, Mount Rainier was in fact a national park. Lying between the park boundary and the Northern Pacific Railway, the Tacoma

In this entertaining advertisement from 1904, the Southern Pacific compares the Wawona Tunnel Tree (true height 227 feet) to the just completed Flatiron Building in New York City (285 feet). Obviously, the height of the tree has been greatly exaggerated, but the railroad has still made its point. Author's collection.

Hoping to exchange high-country scenery for lowland timber, the Northern Pacific Railway shrewdly backed the establishment of Mount Rainier National Park in 1899. From *Wonderland*, 1898. Author's collection.

Eastern remained in an enviable position to develop the tourist traffic. Generally two trains a day were offered, with hundreds of passengers flocking to special trains.

Established in 1902, the nation's sixth national park, Crater Lake, Oregon, lacked the population base of Mount Rainier. Consequently, no branch line was ever built. The Southern Pacific Railroad rather disembarked passengers at Medford, transferring them the remaining eighty-two miles to the park by motor stage. Beginning in 1927, a new main line operating via Klamath Falls and Chiloquin allowed service from the east, for the first time halving the distance to the park but still requiring the motor transfer.

Thus did the Southern Pacific and other railroads look enviably on Grand Canyon, simultaneously under development in Arizona by the Atchison, Topeka & Santa Fe. Led by Yellowstone, the mountain parks were plagued by the problem of visitors traveling only in the summer months. At Grand Canyon, the Santa Fe reasoned, the season might be extended throughout the year. Easterners either headed to California in fall to spend the winter or returning in spring might be convinced to make a stopover. Best of all, in part because Grand Canyon was not yet a national

Established in 1902, Crater Lake National Park, Oregon, was soon a recognized destination of the Southern Pacific Railroad via Medford and eventually Klamath Falls. However, visitation relative to other parks was small. Inevitably, the railroad therefore encouraged recreation (left) before settling on the stunning wilderness portraits of Maurice Logan (right), whose brochure image featuring bears also appeared in the railroad's poster series. *Left:* 9 × 4 inches folded. Courtesy of the California State Library, Sacramento. *Right:* 9 × 8 inches open. Courtesy of Robert Herold.

park, the necessary branch line could go straight to the rim. On September 17, 1901, the sixty-five-mile spur from the main line at Williams, Arizona, ran its first official train. Arriving at the canyon, passengers and officials posed for a picture. El Tovar, the Santa Fe Railway's grand hotel, followed in January 1905. On exiting the train at Canyon Depot, the rim—and El Tovar Hotel—were just moments and steps away.

There remained that one disappointment—Grand Canyon was not yet a national park. Otherwise, the Santa Fe still had a huge advantage. At Yellowstone, the Northern Pacific could offer only a connecting stagecoach between the geyser basins and Gardiner Gateway. In California, the transfer to Yosemite, Sequoia, and General Grant National Parks also required long days on the road.

The Santa Fe Railway's first train to the South Rim of the Grand Canyon, September 17, 1901, was cause for celebration and this official photograph. Courtesy of the National Park Service, Grand Canyon National Park.

Even as Grand Canyon's visitation soared, the Santa Fe Railway still wanted the name. How was the public to recognize the Grand Canyon as the equivalent of Yellowstone without the term *national park*? In 1908, President Theodore Roosevelt proclaimed Grand Canyon a national monument, but a monument still was not a *park*.

Thus had the railroads (and preservationists) discovered the importance of luck and timing. For every national park established quickly, another suffered protracted delays. The proposal for a national park in the Rocky Mountains of Montana similarly encountered both extremes. In the 1880s, the noted explorer and sportsman George Bird Grinnell drew attention to the Montana high country in his magazine, *Forest and Stream*. In 1893, James J. Hill put Grinnell's proposal directly in the path of the Great Northern Railway, which paralleled the Canadian border from Minnesota to Washington State. Railroad access was pivotal, Grinnell also realized. His follow-up article, "The Crown of the Continent," appeared in the September 1901

This charming advertisement appeared in several national magazines in December 1910. The ranger is with the U.S. Forest Service, managing what was then Grand Canyon National Monument. Although the young woman is probably on her way to California, might the handsome ranger have tempted her to stay? 9½ × 6½ inches. Author's collection.

Opened January 14, 1905, El Tovar Hotel (after the Spanish explorer Pedro de Tovar) bore elegant testimony to the Santa Fe Railway's intense interest in Grand Canyon. Painting by Louis Akin (1906), oil on canvas, 25 × 50 inches. Courtesy of the BNSF Railway.

The alpine splendor of Swiftcurrent Lake in Glacier National Park inspired the Great Northern Railway to design the Many Glacier Hotel reminiscent of a lodge in Switzerland. Author's collection.

issue of *Century Magazine*. "Here," he observed, "are cañons deeper and narrower than those of the Yellowstone, mountains higher than those of the Yosemite." A renowned skeptic about the worth of passenger trains, James J. Hill seemed little interested. However, his son Louis, appointed president of the Great Northern in 1907, indeed equated a successful railroad with nearby national parks. Certainly, if Congress approved Glacier National Park, the Great Northern, as the region's only transcontinental railroad, would enjoy a monopoly over arriving passengers.

Grinnell's call for a national park lent further justification to the railway's evolving "See America First" campaign. Why should Americans spend their hard-earned dollars abroad when the Rocky Mountains were comparable to the Alps? Glacier was as beautiful as Switzerland, the railroad argued, and indeed would become the "Switzerland of America." Perhaps even Yellowstone would forfeit some of its visitors (at least, Hill could always hope). In either scenario, it was vital that Glacier

Top: Since 1913, the first impression of Glacier National Park for arriving rail visitors has been this view of Glacier Park Lodge from East Glacier Park Station. The site, which is just outside the park, was purchased from the Piegan Indians. Hileman photograph (79G-29A-1), courtesy of the National Archives. *Above left:* The original interior of the Glacier Park Lodge was a colorful hodgepodge of Native American and Asian motifs, intended to vindicate claims that the Great Northern Railway was a natural gateway to the Pacific Coast and beyond. Hileman photograph (79G-29A-5), courtesy of the National Archives. *Above right:* From 1927, these alpine adventurers colorfully suggest the standard comparisons to Europe, indeed, perhaps now a scene from *The Sound of Music*. Author's collection.

provide what Europe provided (and Yellowstone), namely, good roads and comfortable hotels.

Hill personally would have preferred not to commit the Great Northern Railway to the construction and operation of a hotel chain. In any mountain setting, the railroads were lucky if the tourist season could be stretched past September 1. In Glacier, a June 15 opening was equally problematical. With barely ninety snow-free days a year to amortize all their costs, major hotels in the Rocky Mountains were hard to justify. That said, Hill realized he had little choice. Wealthy tourists expected good accommodations. And because only wealthier Americans could afford the trip, the national parks were no exception. The Great Northern expected to profit by attracting extra passengers to the trains it already had. Simply, if every seat and sleeping berth on the trains could be filled, they would become the source of profit. As Hill noted (and the airlines prove today), the biggest expense was operating the train itself. Once those fixed costs had been paid, every added passenger

As president of the Great Northern Railway, Louis W. Hill (left) was instrumental in the development and promotion of Glacier National Park. Hill poses beside the Glacier Park Lodge at East Glacier Park Station, ca. 1920. Author's collection.

Beginning seasonally in the summer of 1913, the Great Northern added open observation cars to its trains passing through Glacier National Park. Author's collection.

was purely profit. So long as the hotels helped fill the trains—and the hotels at least broke even—his investment in Glacier should pay off.

Besides, with Hill it was also personal. Following standard railroad procedure, he said nothing in public about the park. There is no direct evidence he spoke with Congress. However, within weeks of Glacier's approval on May 11, 1910, blueprints for developing the park magically appeared. The plan was to pattern everything after the lodges and chalets commonly found in Switzerland. Writing for *Collier's* magazine in 1916, the novelist Mary Roberts Rinehart reported enthusiastically on Hill's success. "Were it not for the Great Northern Railway, travel through Glacier Park would be practically impossible." Granted, the railroad was "not entirely altruistic," she admitted, "and yet I believe that Mr. Louis Warren Hill, known always as 'Louie' Hill, has had an ideal and followed it—followed it with an enthusiasm that is contagious."

Two of his backcountry chalets still survive, Sperry and Granite Park, part of the original chain scattered a day apart for hikers and horseback riders. At Belton

From the summer of 1934, this view of East Glacier Park Station at train time finds the westbound *Empire Builder* boarding a good load of passengers. George A. Grant Collection, courtesy of the National Park Service.

(now West Glacier), the restored Belton Chalet recreates the ambiance of 1910. At East Glacier Park Station and Many Glacier Hotel, that ambiance still soars to opulence. Taking advantage of government permission to use native stone and timber, Hill personally supervised the construction of these two major park hotels. At a time when the average laborer made $3 a day, Hill spent $500,000 on each building. "Glacier Park Hotel . . . is almost as large as the National Capitol at Washington," Rinehart wrote, displaying a slight tendency to exaggerate. However, the structure was impressive. Its rustic counterpart at Many Glacier (also on the National Register of Historic Places), further moved her to reaffirm that the Great Northern Railway "has done more than anything else to make the park possible for tourists."

Of course, every western railroad might claim the same. The point about Hill's devotion was the timing. In California, San Francisco now looked for a freshwater supply in the Sierra Nevada—nearly two hundred miles away. The problem for all national parks was the precedent of the city choosing the Hetch Hetchy Valley on the Tuolumne River. Like its larger twin, Yosemite Valley, Hetch Hetchy was well within the confines of Yosemite National Park. The city nonetheless persisted, and in 1913 won approval for its dam and reservoir. Although San Francisco had gained a splendid source for its drinking water, preservationists believed that Yosemite National Park had lost its soul. If even Yosemite could not be saved from encroachment, was any park really safe?

The answer to the wrong development was the right development, meaning tourism, as preservationists soon agreed. In contrast to dams, tourism promised the "dignified exploitation of our national parks," wrote Richard B. Watrous, secretary of the American Civic Association. Wilderness must not be limited to the few. Rather, preservationists needed to publicize "the direct material returns that will accrue to the railroads, to the concessionaires, and to the various sections of the country that will benefit by increased travel." It was either that or invite more raids on the national parks every bit as serious as Hetch Hetchy. Simply, the railroads' historical support for nature remained "essential" as "one of those practical phases of making the aesthetic possible."

In September 1911, a major national parks conference—in fact the first of its kind—addressed the issue at the Old Faithful Inn in Yellowstone. Interior Secretary Walter L. Fisher confirmed the importance of the railroads by inviting them to open the two-day session. Fisher's welcoming remarks were equally heartening, proving that Watrous and his colleagues had been heard. Against the financial obsessions expected of corporations, the railroads practiced a form of "enlightened selfishness." The railroads deserved the country's "grateful recognition" for having advanced the cause of national parks.

Leading off for the railroads, Louis W. Hill then took the podium. "Our relations with the parks are naturally very close, and I believe they should be closer," he began. "Glacier Park in Montana is the most recent of the parks to be created and is the one in which we of the Great Northern are most interested, because our lines touch it, but we are also interested in every national park in the United States. . . . This is because it is practically impossible to sell a round trip ticket to a man for any one park, the public always wanting to go from one park to another." Over the next six years, three identical conferences called by the Interior Department (1912, 1915, and 1917) reaffirmed the railroads' commitment to the development and preservation of national parks.

As immediate proof, the railroads were already engaged in a flurry of national park promotion, collectively spending hundreds of thousands of dollars annually (millions today) on advertising brochures, complimentary guidebooks, and full-page magazine ads. In the East, every railroad also expected to benefit by transferring passengers to the western lines, including three of the latest railroads with national park ambitions, the Rock Island, Chicago, Burlington & Quincy, and Denver & Rio Grande Western. Serving Colorado, all naturally endorsed the establishment

Established in 1915, Rocky Mountain National Park, Colorado, was supported by several major railroads serving nearby Denver. *Left:* The Chicago, Burlington & Quincy joined with the Colorado & Southern to produce this colorful brochure from 1917. 9 × 4 inches folded. *Right:* The Burlington's popular pamphlet for 1925. 9 × 5⅞ inches. Both author's collection.

of Mesa Verde National Park (1906), in the southwestern corner of the state, and Rocky Mountain National Park (1915), sixty miles northwest of Denver.

By 1915, the Burlington also joined in serving Yellowstone, offering a connection via the Cody Road from the east. Arriving at Cody, Wyoming, passengers transferred to motor stages for the sixty-mile drive to Yellowstone, entering the heart of the park over Sylvan Pass. In California, a last major hurdle—direct railroad access to Yosemite—had also been overcome. In September 1905, construction began on

The two original logos of the Yosemite Valley Railroad featured Vernal Falls and El Capitan, here El Capitan. Courtesy of the Yosemite National Park Research Library.

the Yosemite Valley Railroad, following a right-of-way seventy-eight miles east by northeast up the Merced River Canyon from Merced to El Portal (see chapter 5).

In hindsight, the period marked the highpoint of railroad service, both as a means of daily transport and to the national parks. Otherwise, it is hardly a mystery why the railroads supported the parks even when their visitation was unavoidably small. As that visitation grew, so should the number of people taking trains. Because the security of the parks was clearly in numbers, preservationists wanted those increases, too. The unforeseen trend was how many park visitors in the 1920s would permanently switch to the automobile. Only then did the railroads question their investment. For the moment, the alliance was secure. Whether for daily travel or accessing the parks, still all of the magic lay in taking the train.

Covering what is now San Francisco's Marina District, the 1915 Panama-Pacific International Exposition inspired the transcontinental railroads to contribute stunning exhibits on the national parks. In this brochure, the Union Pacific Railroad describes its four-and-a-half acre model of Yellowstone for journalists and travel agents. 7¼ × 5¼ inches. Author's collection.

⚐ FOUR ⚐

The Great Railroad Fair

The Panama Canal is the world's greatest commercial achievement. There is nothing to compare with it and a grand International Exposition to celebrate the realization of this dream of four centuries is eminently appropriate.

—Union Pacific System, *California and the Expositions*, 1915

I believe [in] the creation of a bureau of national parks. I am of the firm opinion that nothing will be achieved, or practically nothing worth while, until we have such a bureau—until we have men in this bureau whose whole time is taken up with matters pertaining to transportation, to hotels, and to the advancement of national parks as a whole.

—James Hughes, General Passenger Agent, Chicago, Milwaukee & Puget Sound Railway, 1912

BEFORE AMERICANS retreated to their television sets and video games, every great national accomplishment called for a fair—a world's fair, as they were known, with one-of-a-kind exhibits and special events. Today, as more Americans withdraw into being spectators, we forget what those fairs were like. Public participation was the key. The fair would be planned and the host city chosen; then, over a minimum of several months, the city would put out the welcome mat. In the railroad age, most visitors came by train and, because their investment

In determining to exhibit Yellowstone, Union Pacific also planned lavish handouts. *Above*: Program brochure with internal map of the park. 5⅝ × 7⅞ inches open. *Opposite page*: Exhibit postcard, 3⅜ × 5½ inches. Both author's collection.

was considerable, planned to stay a week or more. Once on the fairgrounds, people became participants as well as spectators. Today, not even Las Vegas and Disneyland offer anything comparable; at both, entertainment still predominates. Greater than any amusement park, a world's fair was a durable reminder that every American should engage in citizenship.

In 1914, the huge national undertaking represented by the completion of the Panama Canal inspired one of those special celebrations. In fact, two world's fairs were planned, both in California. Now a reality, the canal offered serious competition to the railroads; regardless, all of them planned exhibits. The challenge was how to engage the public without appearing to demean the canal. The solution came in the railroads' focus on the grandeur of the national parks. Why should Americans

EAGLE NEST ROCK   OLD FAITHFUL INN   GOLDEN GATE VIADUCT
Union Pacific System-Yellowstone Park at Panama Pacific Exposition

still believe in railroads? Because the railroads believed in what the Panama Canal could never do, namely, showcasing the American land.

It was indeed the theme by which the railroads seized both celebrations as their own. No doubt, the Panama Canal had revolutionized world trade, more than halving the distance between the Atlantic and Pacific Oceans. Regardless, North America belonged to the railroads. The products of its mines, mills, and factories would always depend on them. People crisscrossing the continent would always need good trains. "One prime objective," the Union Pacific Railroad admitted, announcing its display in San Francisco, "is to show in comprehensive form to the tourist from other sections exactly what the great American West has to offer."

Both fairs would open in 1915. In San Diego, the Panama-California Exposition planned to celebrate "the Spanish idea." Featured exhibits included "broad gardens" and "quiet patios," mission architecture and "Spanish dancing girls." It was not exactly what the railroads had in mind. People with the time to see only one fair would obviously be flocking to San Francisco, where by far the greater venue—the Panama-Pacific International Exposition—was offering a full square mile of space. The investment in the fair, the Union Pacific Railroad advised, foretold the quality of its exhibits. "The cost of the canal is approximately $400,000,000—fully $50,000,000 is expended in the Panama-Pacific International Exposition." Concluded the Union Pacific, now angling to make the sale: "Those who fail to visit

Collector's poster stamps. 1¾ × 2½ inches each. Author's collection.

California this year miss an opportunity the like of which probably will not recur in a lifetime."

Voting their approval, the people of California and the nation passed through the turnstiles eighteen million times, there to be welcomed, just past the main gate, with Union Pacific's four and a half acre model of Yellowstone. Aptly, the railroad's publicist described the exhibit as "titanic," the best of Yellowstone built "true to life." What could be "more appropriate," asked the Union Pacific, "than for the pioneer trans-continental railroad to reproduce this assembling of Nature's grandest awe-inspiring attractions at the Panama-Pacific International Exposition at San Francisco!" Far beyond a model, the railroad noted, "this Yellowstone reproduction is the largest exhibit ever erected at any World Fair, involving the use of two million feet of lumber and the expenditure of half a million dollars."

Yellowstone's famous attractions, featuring Old Faithful Geyser, headed the list of recreated wonders. "At regular intervals, uniform with those of its prototype, great gushes of vast volumes of boiling water and steam are thrown high into the air." Beyond Old Faithful, Yellowstone's Golden Gate, "correct in detail and contour," advised visitors of its special appeal. Next came "Hot Spring Terraces, fed by the water from the Great Falls of the Yellowstone, which pours in a rushing torrent over the lofty precipice with a grandeur akin to the original, possessing irresistible charm." Now sounding like Walt Disney, the Union Pacific Railroad was indeed forty years ahead of its time. "These mountains are certain to prove the most artistic, genuine and real which have ever been attempted in this country or elsewhere. No artificial summits and ranges heretofore produced compare with them in size or effectiveness."

Central to the exhibit, "a novel topographic portrayal" (in fact a giant relief map) provided a bird's-eye view of Yellowstone—showing "the important geyser

From a postcard, this aerial view of the Yellowstone exhibit shows its dimensions and position on the fairgrounds. Alcatraz Island is prominent across the rooftop of Old Faithful Inn. Author's collection.

and other plutonic formations; hot springs, roaring mountains, lakes, falls, cascades, grottoes, government roads, trails and other outlines." No previous exhibit had been "attempted on so large a scale,—somewhat more than one acre in area." Again, credit went to its artists, who, as "enthusiastic lovers of Yellowstone National Park," had brought alive, in miniature, its "remarkable contour, water, river and mountain effects."

In a final stroke of genius, the Union Pacific anchored its exhibit with a full-size replica of Old Faithful Inn. "Old Faithful Inn is conspicuous, well meriting its name. It is not in miniature in any particular, for there is no curtailment in proportions." Rather, like the original, the building covered forty-seven thousand square feet. "Its exterior is, in size and construction, a replica of its prototype in faraway Yellowstone." The reproduction was "exact" in all details. "The hewn-log pillars, railed balconies, multi-gabled roof, and, high above all, the eight flapping pennants, are all there."

The prerequisite change was to the interior. This the Union Pacific had refashioned into a "great banquet hall" seating up to two thousand guests. "The Official Exposition Orchestra, comprising eighty musicians led by a conductor of world-wide fame, holds forth on the stage in the great dining hall of Old Faithful Inn, [with] concerts every afternoon and evening." Special after-dinner concerts were also held.

It was "with certainty," the Union Pacific Railroad therefore predicted, "that this café deluxe with its great orchestra, its cuisine and large floor space for dancing, will be the center of the night life of the Exposition." Adding a final note of pride, "the splendor of Old Faithful Inn," the railroad concluded, "will furnish the setting for the important formal banquets and receptions of the Fair."

Of course, dropping any mention of the Northern Pacific Railway was deliberate. After all, Union Pacific now hoped to convince the fair-going public that West Yellowstone was the superior gateway. The unity among the railroads obviously stopped short of promoting one another's service. However, on the theme of the national parks all agreed. Not only was their beauty a salable item, every exhibit reassured a skeptical Congress that the railroads supported a bureau of national parks. In 1910, J. Horace McFarland, as president of the American Civic Association, had formally addressed the need. In 1912, the word *service* was substituted for *bureau* to quiet the objections of the U.S. Forest Service. Regardless, the Forest Service preferred that

"THE GLOBE" See America exhibit of the Western Pacific–Denver & Rio Grande–Missouri Pacific–St. Louis, Iron Mountain & Southern Lines, located in the northwest corner of the Palace of Transportation, Panama-Pacific International Exposition, San Francisco, 1915. Height of Globe, 44 feet; diameter, 51 feet; extension, 50 x 50 feet. A Bureau is maintained within "The Globe," where illustrated literature and information on any desired district may be obtained. Admission Free.

Visitors to "The Globe" received this complimentary postcard. The back of the postcard reads: "'THE GLOBE,' in the PALACE OF TRANSPORTATION, Panama-Pacific International Exposition, San Francisco." On the outside is a relief map of North America, the largest spherical map in the world, showing the territory served by the lines of the Western Pacific–Denver & Rio Grande–Missouri Pacific–St. Louis, Iron Mountain & Southern. Within is displayed a series of twenty-four illuminated models of cities and towns, mining camps, agricultural districts, industries, and notable scenic points located on the lines of the railroads named." 3⅝ × 5½ inches. Author's collection.

the Park Service die in committee, ending any possible rivalry for control of the public lands. Ever cautious, Congress appeared to agree. Finally, thanks in large part to the Panama-Pacific International Exposition, the bill was back in the spotlight, and that spotlight now impossible to dim.

To be sure, the missing chapter in the evolution of the National Park Service is the critical influence of the fair. Beginning with the Yellowstone Park Conference of 1911, the railroads had repeatedly endorsed the agency. "And it was a very significant thing to me," Interior Secretary Walter L. Fisher reported in a follow-up speech to the American Civic Association, "as I think it will be to you, to find that the Northern Pacific Railroad [sic] Company, whose road leads to one of our principal parks [Yellowstone], was, and is, much in favor, through its representatives, of having a National Park Bureau established." In fact, every principal railroad endorsed the bureau, Fisher observed, having similarly concluded "that it was for their own best interest" to improve conditions in the national parks.

Four years later, at the Panama-Pacific International Exposition, the railroads literally swept the opposition aside. Indeed, Union Pacific's Yellowstone exhibit was just the beginning. In the sprawling Palace of Transportation, four confederate

The Santa Fe Railway's massive indoor diorama of the Grand Canyon included a Pueblo Indian Village on the roof. 3⅝ × 5½ inches. Author's collection.

Great Northern Railway Exhibit Building, Panama-Pacific International Exposition, San Francisco, California

Fairgoers entering the Great Northern Railway Building received this complimentary postcard. The back in part reads: "Visit Glacier National Park. Where mountains surround and beauties abound." Note the Blackfeet Indians greeting visitors. 3½ × 5½ inches. Author's collection.

lines similarly erected a towering, walk-through diorama appropriately named The Globe. "The earth itself is on display," they announced. "The United States, with its mountains, rivers, valleys, national parks and cities, is taken in at a glance. In fact, the eye travels with tiny trains which flit across the huge miniature exactly as the trains they represent are in flight across the continent." The design of the exhibit drew special attention to the number of trains headed for the national parks. "Yellowstone, Mesa Verde, Rocky Mountain and Yosemite National Parks and Great Salt Lake," the railroads confirmed, "are indicated by squares of soft light."

Only the Santa Fe Railway remained disappointed by the absence of Grand Canyon. No matter, its exhibit eclipsed them all. Exceeding the Yellowstone exhibit by an acre and a half, the railroad was modeling Grand Canyon over six acres, all of it indoors. At 30-minute intervals, visitors boarded "an electric observation parlor car," stopping at overlooks along the rim, in all "seven of the grandest and most distinctive points." More than one hundred miles of the canyon were on display, the Santa Fe reported, "reproduced accurately, carefully and wrought so wonderfully that it is hard to realize that you are not actually on the rim of the Canyon itself."

Wherever the visitor turned, a railroad was promoting the national parks. The Southern Pacific filled its palatial building with exhibits of Yosemite and Sequoia. Modeled giant sequoias lined the halls. The Great Northern Railway building

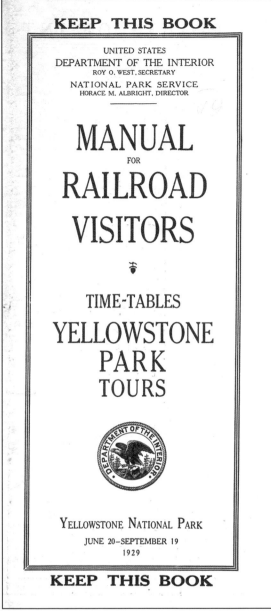

Above left: Stephen T. Mather, as the first director of the National Park Service (1916–1929), worked closely with the railroads as the parks' original corporate allies. *Left:* Recognizing the importance of railroads to Yellowstone, Horace M. Albright, as superintendent (1919–1929), developed a manual for railroad visitors, revised annually. *Right:* The manual cover for 1929. Mather photograph (79-PGN-385) courtesy of the National Archives. Albright portrait courtesy of the National Park Service. Manual 9 × 4 inches folded. Author's collection.

In 1925, the Union Pacific Railroad grandly updated its station complex at West Yellowstone with this magnificent stone dining lodge designed by the architect Gilbert Stanley Underwood. Overnight passengers arriving on the *Yellowstone Special* from Salt Lake City, Ogden, and Pocatello received breakfast before entering the park. Passengers departing on the evening train were served their dinner. At the height of the season, sittings of 350 people each were easily accommodated. Arriving in the afternoon, a second train, the *Yellowstone Express*, was inaugurated in 1922, then permanently dropped after World War II with the falloff in railroad passengers. Courtesy of the Yellowstone Historic Center, West Yellowstone, Montana.

produced "a wonderful display of the beauties of Glacier National Park." Adding a special touch, ambassadors from Glacier's neighboring Blackfeet Reservation, in full ceremonial dress, welcomed visitors at the door.

As a form of cultural lobbying, the Panama-Pacific International Exposition proved a masterpiece. Expressed so creatively and decisively, the need for a National Park Service could no longer be ignored. Established on August 25, 1916, the National Park Service might well have credited its existence to the railroads—and their magnificent fair from the year before.

Because the nation has forgotten its railroads, historians have tended to forget them, too. The popular storyline leading to the National Park Service still focuses on the work of Stephen T. Mather. After the departure of Interior Secretary Walter Fisher, who generously credited the railroads for supporting the national parks, his

The
Great White
Throne
in
Zion National Park
Southern Utah

See This
Colorful Kingdom of Scenic Splendor

**Zion National Park—Bryce Canyon—Cedar Breaks—Red Canyon
Prismatic Plains—Kaibab Forest—North Rim Grand Canyon**

"Unique, incomparable, sublime," says Hal Evarts, the noted writer. Mountains glowing red and shining white. Mile-deep canyons filled with mile-high temples! Canyons holding exquisite fairy cities with countless castles, cathedrals, mosques and pagodas of bewildering beauty, tinted with the colors of a glorious sunset. Prismatic plains, cliff dwellings, enchanting forests alive with deer.

Low summer fares. Complete 450-mile 5-day tour including Kaibab National Forest and North Rim Grand Canyon, or shorter 2 or 3-day tours to Zion, Bryce and Cedar Breaks only. Also escorted all-expense tours. Smooth-riding motor busses. Comfortable lodges. A memorable summer vacation in itself or an easy side trip on tours to Salt Lake City, Yellowstone, California or the Pacific Northwest.

Handsome Book in natural colors tells about this new wonderland in Utah-Arizona. Ask for it.

Address nearest Union Pacific Representative, or General Passenger Agent (Dept. A) at Omaha, Neb. :-: Salt Lake City, Utah :-: Portland, Ore. :-: Los Angeles, Cal.

UNION PACIFIC

Following up on the Panama-Pacific International Exposition, the Union Pacific Railroad undertook the development of Zion and Bryce Canyon National Parks and the North Rim of Grand Canyon National Park. From 1926, this advertisement includes a listing of other popular sights in the region. Painting signed H. Foster. Paper original 9½ × 6½ inches. Author's collection.

The service complement of El Tovar on the South Rim, Grand Canyon Lodge has served the North Rim since 1928. After fire destroyed the main building in 1932, the Union Pacific replaced it with this version, shown here in 1940. The people gathered to the left of the buses are employees singing good-bye to their guests. Courtesy of the Union Pacific Railroad Museum, Omaha, Nebraska.

successor Franklin K. Lane asked for Mather's assistance, later inviting historians to downplay the railroads. Mather himself did nothing of the kind, knowing full well that the railroads remained critical allies. Only more visitors, he agreed with the railroad presidents, would motivate Congress to approve a National Park Service. Meanwhile, he was on the railroads' side. In Arizona, the Santa Fe Railway still chaffed that the Grand Canyon was only a monument and not a park. It should be a park, Mather agreed, and promised it would be when the Park Service was approved.

In 1919, Mather (and Congress) made good on the promise with the establishment of Grand Canyon National Park. Mather's lingering unhappiness lay in the realization that only the South Rim was being served. Then might the Union Pacific Railroad (he pushed a harder sell) similarly agree to develop the North Rim of the canyon?

Because it was Mather asking, the railroad listened. A self-made millionaire from the mining and distribution of borax, he had proved to every railroad his

Guests departing other Utah Parks Company hotels (a subsidiary of Union Pacific) were also treated to employee "sing aways," here performed by the staff of Bryce Canyon Lodge. Courtesy of the Union Pacific Railroad Museum, Omaha, Nebraska.

business acumen. Regardless, the Union Pacific reminded him that building hotels was expensive—especially for a season still barely three months in length. At least, Grand Canyon was finally a national park—along with Zion National Park (originally Mukuntuweap National Monument) in neighboring Utah. In 1924, Bryce Canyon (first known as Utah National Park) cemented the region's popularity. By then, Union Pacific had seen the opportunity, too. It first built a branch line into Cedar City, Utah, to bring passengers as close to the parks as possible. To design the necessary lodges, Union Pacific retained the architect Gilbert Stanley Underwood. A fourth lodge was also constructed in nearby Cedar Breaks National Monument. A major advertising campaign completed the effort, announcing Union Pacific's "Make-Believe Land Come True." Open-air motor stages met the trains in Cedar City, providing circle tours of the parks.

In retrospect, the effort confirmed the staying power of the Panama-Pacific International Exposition. However, even faster than the railroads and Mather had foreseen, millions of Americans were turning to the automobile for both business and pleasure travel. In Utah, the Union Pacific still had the advantage, thanks to

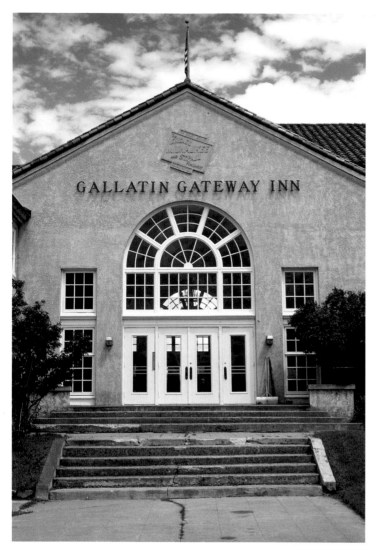

GALLATIN GATEWAY INN

Hoping for closer ties to Yellowstone's family of railroads, the Chicago, Milwaukee & St. Paul Railroad (soon Chicago, Milwaukee, St. Paul & Pacific) turned in 1926 to the development of Gallatin Gateway south of Bozeman, Montana. With the Great Depression just three years away, the effort proved a disappointment, although the Milwaukee promoted new trains and Yellowstone services well into the 1950s. A majestic survivor from the period is the Gallatin Gateway Inn, fully restored as an operating hotel. Trains disembarked passengers behind the inn, where, after an overnight stay, they were bused to West Yellowstone and the park. The original entrance for railroad passengers to the Gallatin Gateway Inn elegantly reminds visitors of its railroad past. Author's photograph is from where the trains arrived.

the relative isolation of that state's major parks. In serving Yellowstone, as a more telling example, the railroads had already lost their historical edge. Early in the 1920s, the Chicago & North Western added a truly distant gateway—Lander, Wyoming—appealing to visitors that they would see Jackson Hole and the Teton Range. Even so, that entire portion was by motor stage over the same roads open to automobiles. Yet a fifth major entrance, the Gallatin Gateway, was developed in 1926 by the Chicago, Milwaukee & St. Paul Railroad. In the process, the Milwaukee built another fabulous railroad hotel, the Gallatin Gateway Inn.

Yet the trend at Gallatin Gateway was also clear. As a company, the Milwaukee had already slipped into bankruptcy, nor did its Yellowstone traffic stem the tide of automobiles. Despite massive publicity efforts, the Milwaukee drew only 6,000 passengers to Gallatin Gateway in 1926. Emerging from reorganization in 1928, it still found itself a minority stakeholder in travel to the park, which,

to Yellowstone Park!

The swift road to happy days

THIS is the logical way to vacationland! The Milwaukee Road reaches all the glorious vacationland of the Northwest by the world-famous *Olympian* or by the *Columbian.*

If you are outward-bound for Alaska, the Far East, or the Islands of the South Seas, it will take you in luxury to shipside on Puget Sound. For 660 miles across four great mountain ranges *it is electrified—the world's longest electrified railroad,* the most modern achievement in smooth, luxurious motion.

If your destination is a favorite vacation spot, undoubtedly The Milwaukee Road leads to it. Gallatin Gateway to Yellowstone. Belt and Ranger Mountains. Rocky Mountains. Upper Valley and sources of the Missouri. Lake Pepin. Lakes and woods of Wisconsin and Minnesota. Bitter Root Mountains. Columbia River. St. Joe River. Lake Chacolet. Mt. Rainier National Park. Cascade Range. Puget Sound. The Olympic Peninsula. The great plains of Montana and the Dakotas. *All reached by trunk lines of the Milwaukee Road.*

The trip on the splendidly equipped *Olympian* is in itself an extraordinary experience. In all the comfort of a fine club you may sweep smoothly through the most diversified, most beautiful, and most interesting regions of America. Perfect service, delicious meals, and an unbroken panorama of stimulating scenes!

MILWAUKEE ROAD

Geo. B. Haynes, Passenger Traffic Mgr.
Chicago, Milwaukee & St. Paul Railway
Union Station, Chicago, Illinois

I am planning a trip ☐ to Yellowstone Park ☐ to the Pacific Northwest. Please send me your travel literature.

Name_____

Address_____

14

A period Milwaukee Road ad (detail) extols Yellowstone via Gallatin Gateway. Author's collection.

Portfolio of Discovery

SEE AMERICA FIRST

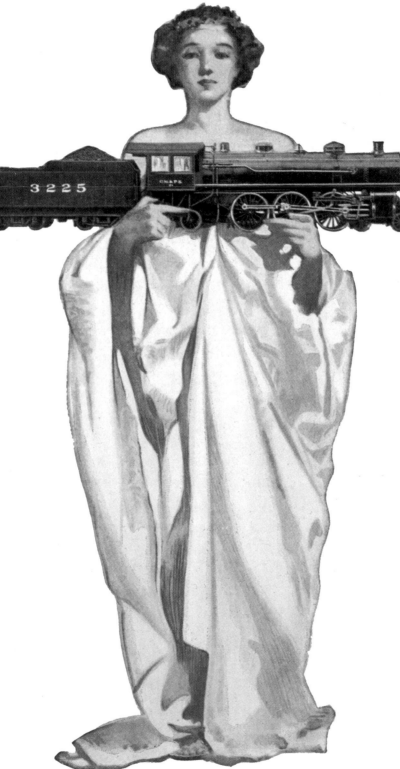

Often attributed to the Great Northern Railway, the See America First campaign dominated the advertising copy of transcontinental railroads on the eve of World War I. The traveling public, the railroads suggested, should be more discriminating and patriotic, that is, willing to spend their dollars on American scenery rather than searching for beauty abroad. At its most fanciful, the See America First campaign inspired many suggestive and colorful images, such as this "Madonna of the Rails," from the title page of the Milwaukee Road's period guidebook, *Across the Continent*. Author's collection.

First commissioned by the Great Northern Railway in 1910, the artist John Fery is renowned for his paintings of Glacier National Park, the Cascade Range, Mount Rainier, and other northwestern scenes. The See America First ideology of the Great Northern is beautifully represented in this large Fery painting, *Mount Index in the Cascades* (Washington State). Note how the railroad blends with its surroundings—an early convention of the Hudson River school. It is as if the

roadbed is but a pathway, effortlessly absorbed by the ancient wilderness. The locomotive, although the center of the painting, is small and indistinct. Depending on one's interpretation, the railroad is nothing to fear or everything to fear, a fleeting incursion on nature or indeed the harbinger of its destruction. Oil on canvas, 47¼ × 83 inches. Courtesy of the BNSF Railway.

BOZEMAN PASS, MONTANA ROCKIES

Companion of Mountains—The North Coast Limited

For more than a thousand miles, the majestic grandeur of Rockies and Cascades accompanies the **New North Coast Limited** through the Northwest, the country pioneered, developed and served by the **Northern Pacific Railway.**

Are you interested in a trip West? May we send our literature? A letter from you will be appreciated. E. E. Nelson, 389 Northern Pacific Railway, St. Paul, Minnesota.

This Album, Free!

The conviction that railroads complement the passing landscape was never more imaginatively conveyed than by the artist Gustav Krollmann. Born and trained in Vienna, Austria, Krollmann emigrated to Saint Paul, Minnesota, where in 1930 he landed a major commission with the Northern Pacific Railway promoting the modernized *North Coast Limited* (facing pages). *Above:* Simultaneously a poster,

menu cover, postcard, ticket envelope, and magazine advertisement (pictured here), the image "Companion of Mountains" (Bozeman Pass, Montana Rockies) is Krollmann's most recognizable work. *Above*: From the same series, locomotive 2607, now in a poster, introduces an idealized view of Mount Rainier from Stampede Pass in Washington State. Advertisement 11 × 8½ inches, poster 40 × 30 inches. Both author's collection

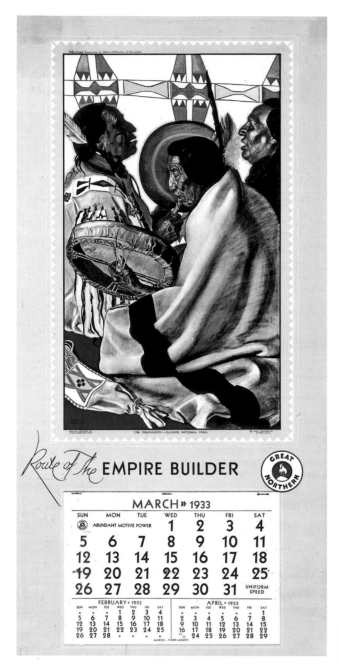

Glacier
national park

Lakes of rarest beauty fed by melt- with highland daisies, lure you onto
ing glaciers, in witchery of reflection the trails that lead to haunts of the
hold towering mountains captive. angler. America's best is the scenic
Meadows of Alpine vastness, radiant West in Glacier National Park.

*Tours via motor, saddle-horse and launch arranged by
day, week and month. Modern hotels and Swiss chalets
offer every comfort. Descriptive literature on request.*

A. J. DICKINSON, *Passenger Traffic Manager*
GREAT NORTHERN RAILWAY
Dept. 29X. St. Paul, Minn.

Early in the twentieth century, it was common to think of Native Americans as a "vanishing race." Led by the Great Northern and Santa Fe railways, several companies generously supported artists' and photographers' efforts to record native cultures before they slipped away. Gradually, the depiction of Native Americans in or near national park settings proved another irresistible cornerstone of the See America First campaign. Invariably, such images were often idealized, as artists strove to commemorate the Indians' pride and endurance in the face of conquest, dispossession, and cultural loss. *Above left: The Drummers—Glacier National Park* by Winold Reiss. Born in Karlsruhe, Germany, in 1883, Reiss stepped off the train at Glacier National Park during a snowstorm in 1919 and began his life's work, in the Great Northern's words, providing "an opportunity to look into the hearts of a people of the past with sympathetic understanding of their sacrifices to the march of civilization." Paper original, 32¾ × 15¾ inches. Author's collection. *Above right:* Original magazine advertisement, 1921. Author's collection.

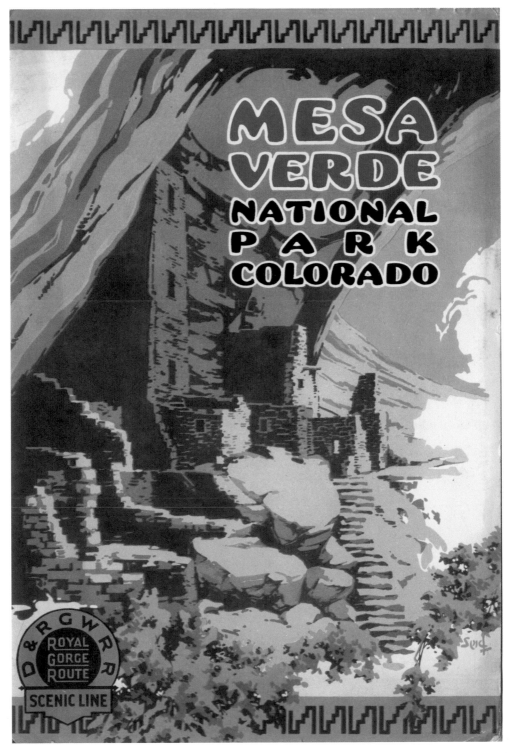

Closely monitored by the railroads, a new awareness that North America had been inhabited for thousands of years before Columbus added to the lure of See America First. Beyond a scenic experience, a railroad journey was also a romantic step back in time. Introducing Mesa Verde National Park, established in 1906, the inside title page of this guidebook by the Denver & Rio Grande Western Railroad promises that "America's sublime antiquity has the lure of a mystery greater than the ruined cities of the old world." 10 × 6¾ inches. Author's collection.

As antiquities made of stone, Zion and Bryce Canyon National Parks offered an unbeatable combination suggesting why Americans should see their country first. Union Pacific took full advantage

BRYCE CANYON

New-Amazing-Sublime

In Bryce Canyon are mammoth amphitheatres of realistic, gorgeously colored sculpture and architecture: queens, princes and potentates, ogres and fairies, ruined Oriental cities, castles and cathedrals of the Middle Ages.

Tremendous colored canyons, colossal buttes, prismatic plains, vast virgin forests, wild horses, countless deer, mysterious cliff dwellings. The most enchanting vacationland is

Zion National Park
Bryce Canyon — Cedar Breaks
Kaibab Forest—Grand Canyon

Easy to reach. Low summer fares. Through Pullmans to Cedar City, Utah, thence 3, 4 or 5-day all-expense motor-bus tours; also escorted tours. Comfortable lodges. Miles of scenic trails for horseback and hiking. A memorable vacation itself or a side trip en route to Yellowstone or the Pacific Coast. Season June 1 to October 1.

The Zion Red Book tells all. Ask for it.

Address nearest representative or General Passenger Agent, Dept. 115, at Omaha, Neb. : Salt Lake City, Utah : Portland, Ore. : Los Angeles, Calif.

UNION PACIFIC
THE OVERLAND ROUTE

in 1927 with these two creative, widely published advertisements. Both 9½ × 6½ inches. Author's collection.

© PRENTISS

Crater Lake, Oregon
Crater Lake National Park

UNION PACIFIC SYSTEM
OVERLAND

As a "captive" venue for promoting the national parks, cross-country trains had no equal. Onboard travelers were encouraged to make national park stopovers with the reminder that the bulk of the cost had already been paid. Hands-on advertising became a specialty of the dining car, where menus, placemats, and coloring books for children told the national park story. In the Union Pacific menu series

Mt. Rainier, Washington
From Spray Park

UNION PACIFIC OVERLAND

represented here (1928–1932), customized covers and descriptions illustrated every major park in the West. *Left*: The menu featuring Crater Lake National Park, Oregon. *Above*: Mount Rainier National Park, Washington. Both 9¾ × 7 inches. Author's collection.

From original painting by ADOLPH HEINZE

THE HIGHWAY NEAR MANY GLACIER HOTEL

This is modern travel in an unspoiled wilderness.
Each mile on these highways opens up new vistas of
beauty and each turn in the road leads to a new
adventure.

Until widespread use of the automobile, travel both at home and abroad was generally limited to the wealthy, for whom the Grand Tour of Europe had long been familiar. In turning the eyes of tourists away from Europe, the success of the See America First campaign depended on assurances that the West was as inviting and no less safe. Railroad timetables, guidebooks, menu covers, company logos—even luggage stickers and ink blotters—were creatively invoked to portray those all-important scenes of accessibility and serenity, of a comfortable wilderness experience in the companionship of fellow travelers. *Above*: A page from the Great Northern Railway guidebook, *The Call of the Mountains*, 1927. Author's collection.

Great Northern Railway luggage sticker, ca. 1925. Diameter 4½ inches. Author's collection.

FROM PAINTING BY THOMAS MORAN

~Grand Canyon, Yellowstone Park

At Your Service

J. P. Roddy, G. A.
H. E. Petersen, C. P. A.
A. C. Stickley, T. P. A.

Our Address

633 Monadnock Bldg.
SAN FRANCISCO
Phone Sutter 1078

YELLOWSTONE PARK — PACIFIC NORTHWEST

1928		MAY				1928
SUN	MON	TUE	WED	THU	FRI	SAT
		1	2	3	4	5
6	7	8	9	10	11	12
13	14	15	16	17	18	19
20	21	22	23	24	25	26
27	28	29	30	31		

The North Coast Limited—One of America's Finest Trains

This evocative painting by Thomas Moran graced one of a series of ink blotters by the Northern Pacific. 9 × 4 inches. Courtesy of the California State Railroad Museum, Sacramento.

The logo of the Tacoma Eastern Railroad (ca. 1910) featured its popular destination, Mount Rainier. Courtesy of the Pacific Northwest Collection, University of Washington Libraries, Seattle.

Longs Peak from Flattop
Rocky Mountain National Park

UNION
PACIFIC
SYSTEM
OVERLAND

Although the railroads, like concessionaires today, were selling the beaten path, See America First did include an appreciation of wilderness, especially for parks with a popular backcountry. *Above*: From the Union Pacific national park series (1930), a menu cover featuring Rocky Mountain National Park

leaves no doubt why a hiker would wish to go there. 9¾ × 7 inches. Author's collection. *Above*: In a Santa Fe Railway poster by the California artist Don Perceval (1949), hikers pause to share the wilderness majesty of Mount Dana on the eastern edge of Yosemite National Park. 24 × 18 inches. Author's collection.

A great new train — THE CALIFORNIA ZEPHYR

Three railroads—the Burlington, the Denver & Rio Grande Western, and the Western Pacific—are placing in operation on March 20th six all-stainless steel trains built by Budd, to provide a new daily service between Chicago and San Francisco over a scenic route of incomparable grandeur.

These are the spectacular new California Zephyrs—trains of almost unbelievable beauty and luxury. Their Vista-Domes, de-luxe coaches, cars reserved for women and children, lounges, diners and most modern of all transcontinental sleepers offer travel enjoyment beyond your dreams.

The California Zephyrs traverse some of the finest scenery in the world, and their schedules, in both directions, permit you to enjoy the most exciting portions during daylight hours . . . the serried peaks of the highest Colorado Rockies . . . Gore and Glenwood Canyons . . . snowy Sierras . . . and California's fabulous Feather River Canyon of gold rush fame.

Another incentive to travel on these wonderful trains is the fact that they are constructed, not merely sheathed, with stainless steel, the strongest material used in building railway cars. Beneath their gleaming surface these cars have structures of the same lustrous metal, three times as strong as ordinary steel. In the United States, the only all-stainless steel cars are built by Budd . . . and Budd builds no other kind. The Budd Company, Philadelphia 32, Pa.

Budd

Beginning in the 1930s and cresting after World War II, America's railroads reinvented the See America First campaign with fabulous new trains and equipment. *Above*: Introduced in 1949, the *California Zephyr* offered the latest cars for observation, known in the trade as vista-domes. The painting is by Leslie Ragan. *Right*: The artist Bern Hill exaggerates the monumental grandeur of the desert Southwest to showcase new locomotives for the *Super Chief*, offering daily 39¾ hour service between Chicago and Los Angeles on the Atchison, Topeka & Santa Fe. Advertisement 14 × 11 inches, poster 24 × 18 inches. Both author's collection.

Always a favorite with the public, bears excited park managers, too, who in the early days, before ecology, encouraged all kinds of promotions depicting bears in human form. Featuring Yellowstone, the transcontinental trains of the Union Pacific excelled in this form of advertising. In the samples here from the 1920s, children are called on to let their imaginations soar. What parent could say no to making a stopover at West Yellowstone after that? Although the National Park Service today properly insists that bears are wild and allows no feeding

Oh, we might fall if we climbed the wall
    Of the Yellowstone Canyon high,
But the Bruins bold go up, I'm told,
    And paint it up to the sky!
They give it a beautiful golden tone,
This wonderful Gorge of the Yellowstone.

and theatrics with any animal, bears remain a timeless example in art and literature of how the national park idea advanced in the American mind. *Left*: The cover of the *Union Pacific's Children's Book of Yellowstone Bears* reprises the famous painting, *The Spirit of '76*, by Archibald MacNeal Willard. The booklet was commonly passed out in the dining car. *Above*: A page from the children's book suggests how the Grand Canyon of the Yellowstone really got its color. Both author's collection.

Beginning in 1923, the Union Pacific Railroad featured bears on its letter-sized foldouts announcing Yellowstone's opening date to travel agents. The images here are by Walter Oehrle, long a commercial artist for the company. In some years, several leaflets were printed and distributed, although the theme was always bears. *Above left:* From 1946, golfer bears "play through" to the gates of West Yellowstone. *Above:* From 1948, an "anchor bear" for the "Union Pacific Radio Corporation" announces Yellowstone's opening June 20. *Left:* Also from 1948, the tourist campaign gets political. *Right:* Combining Yellowstone with neighboring Grand Teton National Park, the last foldout mailed, in 1960, is a hodgepodge of Old Faithful Inn, the Teton Range and Jackson Lake, Jackson Lake Lodge, and the Union Pacific stations at Victor, Idaho, and West Yellowstone, Montana. West Yellowstone will close to passengers at the end of the 1960 season, Victor in 1965. See America First is winding down. All 11 × 17 inches, fully opened, 11 × 8½ inches as shown. Author's collection.

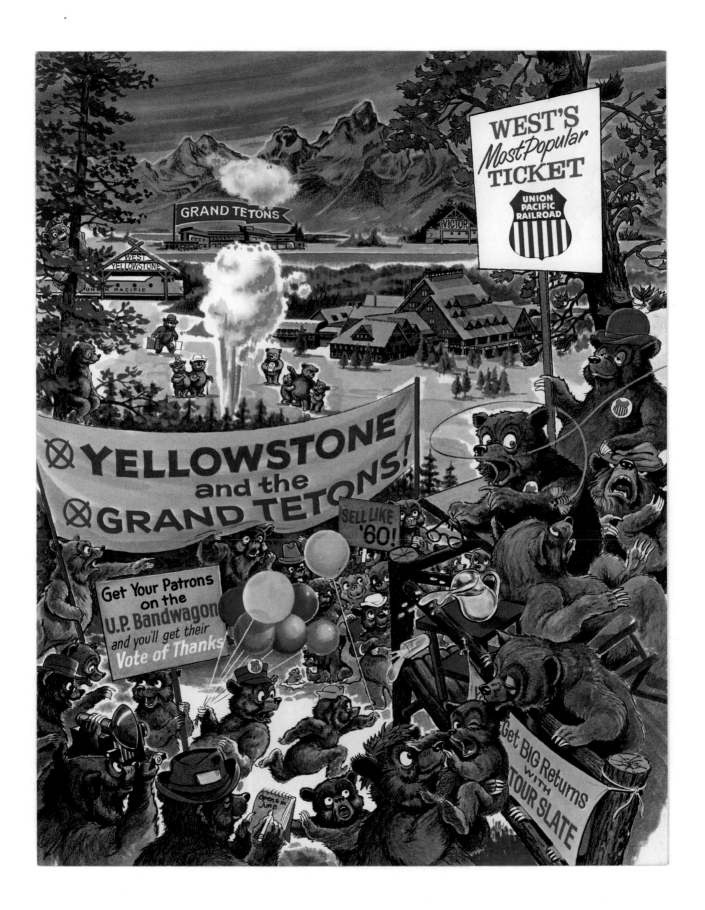

Vol. XIII   MAY 1904   NUMBER I

SUNSET

10 CENTS A COPY   NEW YORK: 349 Broadway   SAN FRANCISCO
ONE DOLLAR A YEAR   CHICAGO: 193 Clark St.   CALIFORNIA
                    LONDON: 49 Leadenhall St.

An illustrious survivor of the See America First campaign, *Sunset* magazine has been in continuous publication since May 1898, when it began in the Passenger Department of the Southern Pacific Railroad. The May 1904 cover featured a painting by the artist Chris Jorgensen, depicting Half Dome and an Indian woman in Yosemite Valley. 9½ × 6½ inches. Courtesy of Bill and Jean Lane.

⚜ FIVE ⚜

Falling Short

THE YOSEMITE VALLEY RAILROAD

Up its matchless canyon this new trail toils, unfolding moment by moment one of the most picturesque series of mountain pictures that nature has fashioned in her whole wide world. This little piece of railroad is sure to take a leading place among the few famous scenic railways of the world.

—Lanier Bartlett, *Pacific Monthly*, 1907

F IN 1915 AMERICA could have foreseen 2015, from climate change to the depletion of oil, logically no railroad would have enjoyed a brighter future than the Yosemite Valley Railroad. Indeed, among rail fans and park enthusiasts alike, few proposals over the years have aroused greater appeal than calls for restoring the line. Granted, some purists might still be opposed. Even on its completion in May 1907, skeptics insisted that a railroad would simply commercialize Yosemite Valley. "In California and the far West, there are people who insist that hereafter the great valley is to be a mere picnic-ground with dancing platforms, beery choruses, and couples contorting in the two-step." So confessed a reporter for *Cosmopolitan* magazine, summing up the belief that "the Black Cavalry of Commerce has been sent out to trample down the fairy rings." Allegedly, such disgruntlement could still be traced to "nature cranks" and the "athletic rich," those resentful that Yosemite was no longer exclusively their domain. "There is the railroad into Yosemite," the

From 1864 to 1907, commercial access to Yosemite Valley was by stagecoach. In this imaginative advertisement using a Yosemite background (February 1907), the Southern Pacific Railroad announces the future. In fact, the opening of the Yosemite Valley Railroad is just three months away. Not only will stagecoaches on the route disappear, their days of valley access are also numbered. 14 × 11 inches. Author's collection.

From 1914, this photograph of the observation car of the Yosemite Valley Railroad was widely featured in company advertising. Courtesy of the Yosemite National Park Research Library.

reporter concluded, declaring democracy victorious, "and all the arguments since Adam and Eve will not put it away."

The railroad actually did not enter the valley proper, or for that matter the national park. This remains the singular differential between railroads in Europe and the United States. In Europe, railroads are considered permanent; once built, they are rarely displaced by highways. In Europe, the Yosemite Valley Railroad likely would have survived when the highway paralleling it was improved. Instead, the railroad was gone in less than forty years. Today, only crumbling embankments lining the Merced River remind us that a railroad was ever there. In Europe, its survival would have been a priority, just as here its bankruptcy was an excuse to scrap it. Consequently, when planners today "plan" Yosemite, they play musical chairs with parking lots. Simply, American culture dares not admit the contradiction of allowing one technology to displace another.

Certainly, the automobile, from sprawl to pollution, has proved the greater threat to natural areas. In Yosemite Valley, one square mile (and there are only seven) has been given over to development. Europe saw the contradiction and dealt with it, as necessary, banning cars from mountain valleys and historic city centers. Public transportation remained the compromise for allowing access while protecting landscape.

Absent a similar commitment in Yosemite, the demise of the Yosemite Valley Railroad was inevitable. From the start, the railroad existed for but two reasons—exporting logs and importing tourists. In February 1905, the actual reduction of Yosemite National Park finally made the railroad viable. All told, 542 square miles—much of it rich in timber—were eliminated from the park. Even as the railroad gradually lost passengers to the automobile, it continued to compensate with logging shipments, until, by the late 1920s, the forests themselves were running out.

Europe's equivalent of Yosemite Valley—the spectacular Lauterbrunnen Valley in Switzerland—is instructive of why the Yosemite Valley Railroad was not preserved. In Europe, the issue of scarcity had arrived centuries earlier. Lauterbrunnen Valley, in the Bernese Alps, had been settled since the 1300s. Consequently, Europe considered railroads, no less than cathedrals, a permanent fixture on the landscape. The expense of replacing railroads by duplicating them with highways was rejected from the start. Let the highway also prove itself, Europe insisted, before we destroy the investment we have already made. Lauterbrunnen therefore kept its railroad. In a country educated by density and centuries of scarcity, railroads were just too important to remove for cars.

In contrast, the United States rejected scarcity as un-American. The logical progression was from old to new. Only new technologies should be advanced. Besides, railroads were too controlling—and restrictive. If necessary, the *number* of people entering Yosemite Valley should be limited, not anyone's right to drive. In either case, railroads as the older technology were immediately suspect as incapable of advancing progress.

Thus the Yosemite Valley Railroad ended where its capabilities ended, stopping twelve miles short of the valley at El Portal. In Switzerland, a cog-assisted roadbed would have completed the journey. The railroad would not have been artificially limited but rather allowed to meet its namesake. Like Lauterbrunnen, Yosemite Valley would have been "invaded" by slivers of railroad but spared the invasiveness of roads and parking lots.

El Portal station, the gateway to Yosemite, at train time, ca. 1916. Arriving passengers transfer across the platform to motor stages for the remaining one-hour-and-thirty-five-minute trip to Yosemite Valley proper. Courtesy of the Yosemite National Park Research Library.

It was too much foresight for 1907—a year with just ten thousand visitors, and that even with the coming of the railroad. Meanwhile, with no real competition yet in sight, the Yosemite Valley Railroad could only thrive. Suddenly, what had been a two-day trip over substandard roads by stagecoach became just four hours on the train. Arriving from Los Angeles and San Francisco, the Southern Pacific Railroad added sleeping-car service direct to El Portal. First-class passengers need only board their trains in either city, snuggle comfortably into their berths, and wake up at El Portal, their sleeping car having been transferred to the Yosemite Valley Railroad at Merced. A parlor-observation car delighted passengers on the daytime run and, during the summer season, the railroad added a full-sized diner.

By 1916, the railroad was averaging 14,000 passengers annually, indeed an important milestone. However, a disquieting shift was already noticeable. Eschewing the round-trip fare of $18.50, slightly more people had come by car. The phenomenon obviously portended problems if the railroad could not compete by entering the park itself. Nor was that possibility even mentioned, again, the United States

Pullman Service *All the Way*

YOSEMITE CARS

The end of your railroad journey and the entrance to the magic valley — that is El Portal. Here is the terminal station of Yosemite Valley Railroad, a distinctive rustic structure blending admirably with the rugged setting.

As the train nears Yosemite Valley, the view becomes ever more magnificent. Just before reaching El Portal—the river rushing by at our feet—in the hazy distance, a silvery shimmering streak breaking the rugged cliffs. It is Chinquapin Falls, first to be seen of the waterfalls of Yosemite—a promise of the scenic glories soon to be unfolded.

YOSEMITE VALLEY RAILROAD CO.

This page from the 1928 Yosemite Valley Railroad brochure, "Yosemite via Merced Canyon Route," features the station platform at El Portal. Courtesy of the Yosemite National Park Research Library.

Destroyed by fire on October 27, 1917, the railroad's Del Portal Hotel was never replaced. Courtesy of the Yosemite National Park Research Library.

not being Switzerland. By 1917, the railroad's passenger count had plummeted to 8,612, a decline of 40 percent in just one season. In 1918, the decline was even worse. Fewer than 4,000 people rode the train, despite every effort to attract more passengers, including a reduced fare of $15.50.

In contrast, 26,669 people entered Yosemite Valley by car, up from 14,527 and 22,456 in 1916 and 1917, respectively. Clearly, the American love affair with the automobile had begun. Nor did the National Park Service, eager to secure its future, have any intentions of cooling the romance. In Congress, every request for new appropriations came with the question whether more visitors were being served. With private cars soaring in popularity, supporting only trains would have immediately discredited the agency. "The fact that the majority of people entering the park came in private automobiles," Yosemite's superintendent reported in 1917, "is evidence that it is this class of travel that must be given the bulk of consideration in future park development work." Specifically, "roads and public parking places must be given special consideration by the Service, and garage facilities and hotel and camp accommodations which appeal to this class of travel must be maintained by the concessioners."

With the completion of the Yosemite Valley Railroad, two major transcontinental railroads, the Southern Pacific and Santa Fe, offered direct connecting services through their stations in Merced. From the 1910s and early 1920s, these colorful brochures alerted prospective passengers. *Far left:* Courtesy of the Bancroft Library, University of California,

Berkeley. *Middle left:* Courtesy of the Huntington Library, San Marino, California. *Middle right:* Courtesy of the California State Library, Sacramento. *Far right:* Courtesy of the Yosemite National Park Research Library.

At least in 1917, that assessment also appealed to preservationists. No one foresaw that Yosemite would close the twentieth century averaging between three and four million visitors per year. The problem in 1917 was still a lack of patronage. True, the railroad had doubled Yosemite's visitation, but the number doubled was just five thousand. Even with ten thousand visitors annually, Yosemite was not secure. By then, preservationists everywhere feared for the integrity of the national parks. Congress was not likely to support them indefinitely for the benefit of the rich. Even if opponents used that argument simply hoping to develop parks, the charge of elitism needed a credible answer.

Geography only compounded the problem. Every national park was still in the West, far removed from the centers of population in the East. Only the railroads covered those distances swiftly and comfortably, but again, not within the budget of average Americans.

In contrast, the automobile promised to "democratize" long-distance travel. Finally, all of the parks would be accessible to what Americans increasingly described as the middle class. The security of the national parks would be greatly strengthened, both politically and economically. Mounting physical threats to the national parks, principally dams, power lines, and reservoirs, further underscored the necessity of compromising some wilderness to accommodate public access. Either preservationists conceded the necessity of roads and cars, or Congress would force the parks to live with worse. In the end, it was a matter of integrity versus practicality. Without some concessions to civilization, the survival of nature had little chance.

Temporarily, the return of national prosperity following World War I softened those concerns. Leisure travel boomed, and with it the success of America's railroads. Between 1921 and 1925, the Yosemite Valley Railroad averaged twenty thousand passengers annually, an all-time high. Brighter years had to be ahead.

However, by 1928 the number of passengers had fallen again—this time by a whopping 80 percent. Nor did another fare cut stem the decline. As promised, the new All-Year Highway, completed in 1926, made auto travel to the park a breeze. As ominous, the railroad's primary source of business—logging—was coming to an end. After twenty years of intensive cutting inside what had been the original boundary of the park, the great stands of sugar pine were running out.

Ultimately, the Great Depression sealed the railroad's fate. In 1935, the railroad saw no choice but to declare bankruptcy and reorganize. Disaster overtook the reorganization in December 1937 when the Merced River flooded and spilled its banks, washing out whole sections of the line. It was one calamity too many. Despite accusations that the railroad was covertly profitable, in 1944 its owners petitioned the Interstate Commerce Commission for abandonment.

By then, Yosemite visitation, too, had slowed to a trickle, undermined by the demands of World War II. Regardless, two official protests made noteworthy mention of what the railroad still meant to the park. Defending preservation, O. A. Tomlinson, regional director of the National Park Service, and Michael W. Straus, acting secretary of the interior, remained convinced the railroad should be restored. Straus personally urged the Interstate Commerce Commission to consider "public convenience and necessity." Abandoning the railroad would jeopardize both. Quoting Director Tomlinson, the government would be taking a "backward" step, Straus concluded. Once the war had ended, the number of vacationing Americans was bound to increase, in which case "the Yosemite Valley Railroad can perform a needed and valuable service in taking care of visitors to Yosemite National Park."

Unfortunately, with World War II still raging in the Pacific, too few current passengers proved the argument. In peacetime, it seemed equally probable that more Americans would simply buy a car. The Interstate Commerce Commission agreed with the railroad and, in June 1945, granted its petition for abandonment. Its final trains ran in August. Henceforth, the Yosemite Valley Railroad would live on only in memories tinged with nostalgia and regret.

To be sure, rail enthusiasts still lament the chain of events that cost them one of their favorite mountain railroads. Preservationists would also come to see its abandonment as a significant loss. In 1954, annual visitation to Yosemite topped one million for the first time in its history. In 1967, two million people entered the park. Exacerbated by the confines of the valley floor, it seemed that auto-based development had finally gotten out of hand.

In 1968, the Park Service launched its first reforms, permanently ending the historic firefall as an evening spectacle for valley visitors. In season, thousands had gathered in the meadows to watch the huge bonfire cascade over the cliff at Glacier Point. Correspondents likened the crush of people to a carnival, complete with litter, blaring radios, and after-show traffic jam. Although a century-old tradition, the firefall was hardly a natural feature, calling simply for a big rake pushed against a pile of embers. It should be stopped, the Park Service agreed, and the virtual grandstand in Stoneman Meadow returned to its natural state.

A second reform in 1970 closed the eastern third of the valley to motor vehicles. In cooperation with the park concessionaire, the Park Service provided a system of free shuttle buses instead. Although modest by modern standards, it was a revolutionary step at the time. Rarely had cars been restricted anywhere in the United States, and especially in the national parks. The object of transportation, hikers and bicyclists insisted, should be to enhance the park experience. Certainly, no one preferring to walk should feel intimidated by endless strings of oncoming cars.

In 1975, a final reform invited the public to comment on a new management plan for Yosemite. The Park Service itself was in for a big surprise. On the issues of congestion and overcrowding, fully 29 percent of the seventy-five thousand respondents supported restoring the Yosemite Valley Railroad. Strategically, the Park

Merced Canyon, the Approach to Yosemite Valley, California.

As senior Park Service officials agonized in 1945, the loss of the Yosemite Valley Railroad, shown here in an original period postcard, cost Yosemite Valley a viable option for limiting automobiles. 3½ × 5½ inches. Author's collection.

Service downplayed the statistic, noting the difficulty of rebuilding the railroad, not to mention extending it to the valley. New parking lots were instead proposed, allegedly to be set unobtrusively in the west end of the valley or somewhere just outside. Then what about hikers along the rim looking down on the valley? asked opponents. The cars could not possibly be screened from so high above. Was not the problem—too many motor vehicles period—simply being put off for a later day?

With or without public transportation, Yosemite's visitation was bound to grow—and did, cresting at four million in 1994. A major flood three years later brought the first reprieve in more than fifty years. Even so, it was a negative reprieve, officials admitted, in that the flooding was hardly planned.

Simply put, yesterday's future has arrived. Must every park keep its roads? If admittedly a railroad is also development, it at least minimizes so many others. On trains, people limit their footprint rather than widen it. That is what Europe knows.

Once upon a time in Yosemite, there was a railroad to El Portal. In Switzerland, such a railroad still exists. Lauterbrunnen is developed and Yosemite Valley still a wilderness, or so we Americans would like to think. The truth is that both are developed, and Yosemite Valley perhaps more so, considering its lost tranquility. The car is freedom, but it is not tranquility. Only its railroad ever promised Yosemite that.

The loss of wilderness hundreds of years ago has prompted different attitudes throughout western Europe. In Switzerland's Yosemite, the Lauterbrunnen Valley, mountain railroads invite all visitors to leave their cars behind. Might a similar emphasis on public transportation better preserve our national parks and natural areas? Photograph by the author, June 1982.

TITAN of CHASMS
Grand Canyon of Arizona

Departing the main line of the Santa Fe Railway at Williams, Arizona, the sixty-five-mile Grand Canyon branch served the South Rim until 1968. A first tourist publication, *Titan of Chasms*, appeared shortly after the railroad's opening in 1901. For the cover of the 1915 edition, the railroad used a painting by the artist William Robinson Leigh. Original paper edition, 9¼ × 6½ inches. Author's collection.

⚜ SIX ⚜

Return to Grand Canyon

When I first heard of the Santa Fe trains running to the edge of the Grand Cañon of Arizona, I was troubled with thoughts of the disenchantment likely to follow. But last winter, when I saw those trains crawling along through the pines of the Coconino Forest and close up to the brink of the chasm at Bright Angel, I was glad to discover that in the presence of such stupendous scenery they are nothing. The locomotives and trains are mere beetles and caterpillars, and the noise they make is as little disturbing as the hooting of an owl in the lonely woods.

—John Muir, *Century Magazine*, November 1902

ALMOST WITHOUT exception, Americans judge the value of any technology foremost in terms of age. Newer is better—indeed must be better—or so most Americans still confidently believe. Given that bias, the revival of the Grand Canyon Railway on September 17, 1989, seems all the more remarkable. To be sure, the twenty-year dream to restore the famous branch line ran counter to the opinions of many "experts." The public, it was commonly argued, preferred automobiles over trains. Few people would ride a train to the Grand Canyon if cars were still allowed. The passenger train—any train—was old-fashioned and too slow. The future of American transportation was still modern highways and expanding airlines.

As that argument crested in the 1960s, railroads abandoned even their most famous passenger trains. Citing its own declining patronage, in 1968 the Atchison,

El Tovar overlooks the first passenger train in twenty-one years to arrive at Grand Canyon Depot, September 17, 1989. An excited crowd has just enjoyed the official ceremonies. Photograph by the author.

Topeka & Santa Fe Railway discontinued passenger service between Williams, Arizona, and Grand Canyon National Park. Officially abandoned in 1974, the historic branch line was in danger of being scrapped. The few people asking perennially that it be restored considered themselves true environmentalists. If the Park Service was serious about limiting automobiles at Grand Canyon, there was no better option than the railroad.

All that the proposal lacked was sufficient capital. Unfortunately, new investors kept stepping forward only because the old ones had disappeared. Suddenly (and many would say miraculously) the problem of capital was overcome. In March 1987, even as crews were preparing to scrap the tracks, two Phoenix investors, Max and Thelma Biegert, purchased and reorganized the line as the Grand Canyon Railway. Its restoration would begin immediately, they announced. A second announcement in January 1989 confirmed that passenger service would resume in April 1990. Accordingly, a final announcement brought exciting news—the actual opening

Earlier on September 17, the opening ceremony in Williams featured the renowned Arizona artist Fred Lucas, who presented the state with an original painting for the capitol building. Photograph by the author.

would be eight months earlier. The new reinaugural date was to be September 17, 1989, exactly eighty-eight years to the day since the first Santa Fe passenger train had arrived at the South Rim.

As crews rushed to meet the new deadline, it seemed an impossible task. Portions of the sixty-five-mile route needed extensive rehabilitation; the entire track needed new rails and ties. Simultaneously, the railroad had purchased two historic steam locomotives now waiting to be restored. Masons and carpenters were also needed at the combination Harvey House and depot in downtown Williams, which, after restoration, was to retain the name Fray Marcos. Antique passenger coaches obtained from the Southern Pacific Railroad were to complete the restoration, each rebuilt to reflect the heyday of the Grand Canyon Railway during the 1910s and 1920s.

Amazing themselves as much as the public, the restorers pulled it off. As the morning of September 17, 1989, dawned, not even the clouds could darken a day so filled with gratitude for the Biegerts' accomplishment. Having nearly lost the

Loaded with passengers, the restored *Williams Flyer* approaches Grand Canyon National Park. Early estimates concluded that the railroad reduced congestion by twenty-five thousand motor vehicles annually. By 2010 those estimates had increased fourfold. Photograph by Al Richmond, courtesy of the Grand Canyon Railway.

railroad, Arizona owed them an incredible debt—as did every business in downtown Williams, effectively bypassed by Interstate 40. Even so, the presence of a train in the station was still hard to comprehend. Braving the intermittent showers, two thousand people pressed forward to hear if the dignitaries then knew to say it. The day was incredible, not only memorable. Also at Grand Canyon National Park, cars would be giving way to preservation. In the end, the dignitaries did respond, turning to Fred Lucas, an Arizona artist, to bring the ceremony full circle. The railway's rein-augural, he confirmed, was part of a greater legacy. Beyond promoting the canyon, the railroad had protected it. He believed in the railroad as the best protector still. Through the gift of its restoration, the state and the nation had found their missing voice. Adding his voice, he was pleased to donate a large painting to hang in the Arizona state capitol. A century of artists, many commissioned by the railroad, had confirmed the importance of the canyon's naturalness. Only the latest artist to represent the history, he looked forward to rebuilding the mission, too.

The ceremonies completed, the first of the restored steam locomotives coupled to the long string of waiting coaches. Six hundred people, guests of the Biegerts, had been invited to take the train. North of Williams, thousands more lined the tracks. Another four thousand waited expectantly at Canyon Depot and El Tovar. There the train's arrival called for another round of speeches and the driving of a golden spike. A final promise elated cultural historians—Canyon Depot was also to be restored.

As the day ended, the train returned to Williams, pacing the glow of a radiant twilight. A hush fell over the coaches at this benediction to an amazing trip. A historic railroad had been reborn instead of thoughtlessly abandoned. Grand Canyon would not suffer the fate of Yosemite and a railroad falling short, or, as in the case of Yellowstone, lose two major railroad entrances. America would not be repeating those mistakes. To be sure, never had there been a better opportunity to save Grand Canyon while teaching other parks to follow its lead.

A quarter century later, the Grand Canyon Railway is averaging 225,000 riders and displacing as many as 100,000 cars per year. It is the basis, preservationists contend, for eventually removing all motor vehicles from the rim, perhaps by building a light-rail system or increasing service out of Williams.

Thanks to the Grand Canyon Railway, the question is posed every day. If cars are allowed in the national parks, why are they allowed? Asphalt is as permanent as any railroad, and yet it is our railroads we accuse of being inflexible. Does the car anywhere encourage preservation? Beginning September 17, 1989, three million train riders have faced up to that question. It was a memorable day for the nation indeed.

Depicted here after its modernization in 1947, the *Empire Builder* has provided continuous service to Glacier National Park since 1929. Courtesy of Richard Piper.

❦ SEVEN ❦

Discovery Today

The decimalization of the American vacation into 4.1 nights will be regarded by Europeans as further evidence of cultural collapse. . . . Americans have tragically deserted the most heroic dimension of their own continent: size. With many other Europeans, I feel that Americans are strangers to their own country in a way that no European can be. One reason is the demise of the American railroad.

—Clive Irving, *Condé Nast Traveler*, September 1992

FOR DECADES, the American vacation has been growing shorter, until many no longer recognize it as vacation. Although older Americans still believe in long vacations, our friends abroad have a point. We are obsessed with saving time. We are more likely to fly than take a train, finding the continent still in our way. Even when driving we see practically nothing of the real America lying just beyond the interstate. As our children grow bored, automakers seem to think we should keep them quiet by playing a DVD. The latest cars even come with built-in monitors. In the end, no one watches the passing countryside, even if it is only to count the billboards.

In the past, travel was all about enjoying the landscape. Although less and less of wilderness remained, rural America could be beautiful, too, and there were always the national parks.

The following national parks and historical sites are where that relationship still endures. The criterion is proximity; generally, the park and its railroad are right next door. The few without scheduled rail passenger service are included with the confidence that one day their trains will be restored. In short, these are the true railroad gateways between civilization and the national parks, hopeful reminders that the word *vacation* can still mean the joy of slowing down.

STEAMTOWN NATIONAL HISTORIC SITE— SCRANTON, PENNSYLVANIA

Once pivotal to the operations of the Lackawanna Railroad, Scranton remains at the heart of a regional landscape uniquely imprinted by its railroad builders. For visitors, that history comes alive at Steamtown. The former shops and roundhouse of the Lackawanna Railroad, Steamtown became a national historic site in 1985. Although some historians at the time were skeptical, Steamtown has proved itself a worthy representative of railroading nationwide. After all, as would be the case in any railroad museum, the "museum" is the country itself. The uniqueness of

The engine house roundtable at Steamtown National Historic Site excites visitors young and old. Courtesy of the National Park Service at Steamtown. Photograph by Ken Ganz.

Steamtown is how it engages the visitor to understand the larger history. An environmental interpretation of American railroading could hardly ask for a better site. As noted in chapter 1, these Pennsylvania mountains and valleys originally inspired the railroads to think of landscape in the first place.

North of Scranton, that history unfolds at Lanesboro, the site of the Starrucca Viaduct. In 1846, the New York & Erie Railroad faced a yawning valley pierced by Starrucca Creek. Engineers decided to leap the valley over a great viaduct built of native rock. The material chosen was Pennsylvania bluestone, cut from an adjacent hill. In recent years, quarrying on the hill has resumed. The viaduct proper, completed in 1848, stands as testimony to that earlier age when Pennsylvania bluestone was more than a popular ornament for garden patios. Thrust skyward as a magnificent bridge, bluestone evolved into memorable art. Painted in 1865 by Jasper Francis Cropsey and in 1951 by Bern Hill, Starrucca Viaduct remains a stunning reminder of how the railroads were once built for beauty.

Twenty-five miles southwest, the Tunkhannock Viaduct, in sustaining such beauty for the town of Nicholson, uses ten graceful arches spanning nearly half a mile. From 240 feet, the view by train was promoted on every daylight run. When completed in 1915, Tunkhannock Viaduct capped a massive modernization effort undertaken by the Lackawanna Railroad. All told, more than a hundred miles of right-of-way were leveled and straightened, cutting at least twenty minutes from the schedule between Buffalo and New York. Most important, one or two locomotives pulling a train through the mountains could finally substitute for three or four. Operating costs were slashed overnight. The railroad then celebrated the Tunkhannock Viaduct as the greatest concrete bridge in the world, the perfect engineering wonder to complement the natural landscape, as originally popularized by Phoebe Snow.

By then, the Lackawanna's new Beaux-Arts station in downtown Scranton had also drawn rave reviews. Opened in 1908, the palatial waiting room perfected the art of anticipation. "Probably its most striking decorative feature is the thirty-six faience panels in colors after the painting of Clark G. Vorhees, the well-known landscape artist," the railroad's publicist reported. "These panels were reproduced in color direct from Nature and represent actual scenes along the line of the Lackawanna Railroad." The mood was heightened by placing the panels above eye level, encircling all four walls. The nuance asked passengers to keep looking up, celebrating not only the scenery but also the railroad. In art or life, no railroad more embodied the cradle of American civilization, from Niagara Falls to the Delaware Water Gap, capped imperially by the skyline of New York.

Although not directly a part of Steamtown, the station is perhaps its most important partner, now the Radisson Lackawanna Station Hotel. Scranton lost its last passenger train in January 1970, ending the station's ties both east and west.

In *Wilderness Threshold* by J. Craig Thorpe, the *Empire Builder*, now under Amtrak, pauses at East Glacier Park Station. Little changed in a century, the combination of station, lodge, train, and historic red buses makes for a fabulous cultural resource. Oil on canvas, 18 × 24 inches. Courtesy and permission of the artist.

Designated Waterton/Glacier International Peace Park in 1932, the units are managed separately, although still in recognition of their common scenery and wildlife populations.

For soaking up the historical ambiance, nothing beats staying in a park hotel, again, one originally constructed under the auspices of the Great Northern Railway. These are Glacier Park Lodge at East Glacier (1913), Many Glacier Hotel on Swiftcurrent Lake (1915), and the equally stunning Prince of Wales Hotel at Waterton Lakes, Canada (1927). Built separately in 1914, Lake McDonald Lodge joined the railroad's holdings in 1930, after which the Great Northern renovated the property. "The original building," the railway reassured patrons, "still provides accommodations of rustic charm and beauty."

Partners in Preservation by J. Craig Thorpe. One of Glacier's celebrated railroad neighbors, the Izaak Walton Inn is renowned for backcountry access, recreation, and interpretation. Also open year-round, it invites visitors who prefer the park off-season. Commissioned by the inn, this winter painting of the arriving *Empire Builder* indeed reminds us that the wonder of Glacier never stops, even when the park is officially closed. Oil on canvas, 18 × 24 inches. Courtesy of the Izaak Walton Inn and permission of the artist.

The perfect complement to the *Empire Builder* and the historic hotels is the fleet of motor stages operated by Glacier Park, Inc. Instantly recognized in their dazzling livery (bright red with jet black fenders), classic originals date from 1936. Hope for sunshine, a nip in the air, and Glacier's brilliant blue skies, all motivation for your driver to break out the woolen blankets and roll back the canvas covering.

Make sure your tour includes Going-to-the-Sun Road, the park's spectacular transmountain highway. Heading west to east, the road parallels Lake McDonald and rushing McDonald Creek, ascends the Garden Wall, crosses windswept Logan Pass (elevation 6,649 feet), and drops again to the shores of majestic St. Mary Lake, all within fifty miles.

At Essex, the Izaak Walton Inn is another nostalgic park experience, and the only hotel offering full accommodations throughout the year. Your shuttle is waiting as you disembark the *Empire Builder*, which stops just a quarter mile away. In summer, a full complement of activities includes white-water rafting, guided hikes, and all-day tours. In winter, miles of groomed trails lure cross-country skiers from Canada, Europe, and the United States. Other visitors come just to enjoy the hotel. Originally constructed as a railroad dormitory in 1939, it remains a refuge suggesting home. The scale is spacious but disarmingly intimate. On summer afternoons, guests begin gathering on the porch just to delight in watching trains. Year-round, picture windows the length of the dining room also provide a great view of the tracks. Watch for helper engines emerging from the adjacent siding to assist heavy freights headed east over Marias Pass.

The latest restoration, Belton Chalet at West Glacier, is truly the original reminder of Glacier's founding—preceding even the great hotels. Louis W. Hill, as president of the Great Northern Railway, personally launched the set of buildings as the first in his chalet and hotel chain. His chosen location, just opposite the station, helped further publicize the railroad's role. The walk today is divided by Highway 2, although traffic is light when the trains arrive. Just to the east, the highway and railroad diverge, the railroad following John Stevens Canyon beside the Middle Fork of the Flathead River. By far the more scenic passage (check the cover of this book) is the one by train.

For More Information

Glacier National Park: Write the superintendent, Glacier National Park, West Glacier, Montana 59936. Or call 1-406-888-7800.

Cooperating Association (guidebooks, trail guides, seminars, and other specialized information): Write the Glacier Association, P.O. Box 428, West Glacier, Montana 59936. Or call 1-406-888-5756.

Park Lodging and Guided Tours: Call Glacier Park, Inc., at 1-406-892-2525. From Canada the number is 1-403-236-3400. Or write to Glacier Park, Inc., P.O. Box 147, East Glacier, Montana 59434-0147 (May–September address), or 1850 N. Central Avenue, Suite 800, Phoenix, Arizona 85004-4545 (October–April address).

Izaak Walton Inn: Write 290 Izaak Walton Inn Road, Essex, Montana 59916. Or call 1-406-888-5700.

Belton Chalet: Write P.O. Box 206, West Glacier, Montana 59936. Or call 1-888-235-8665.

GRAND CANYON NATIONAL PARK—ARIZONA

Gateway Train: **Williams Flyer** (Grand Canyon Railway). For reservations call 1-800-THE-TRAIN (1-800-843-8724). The Grand Canyon Railway provides a shuttle connecting at Williams Junction with Amtrak's *Southwest Chief.* For Amtrak reservations call 1-800-USA-RAIL (1-800-872-7245).

Service Frequency: Grand Canyon Railway, daily except Christmas Eve and Christmas Day; Amtrak, daily (subject to change).

Arrival: The *Williams Flyer* makes one stop in Grand Canyon National Park, at the historic Grand Canyon Depot (El Tovar Hotel, Bright Angel Lodge, Maswik Lodge, Yavapai Lodge).

Principal Departure Cities: The *Williams Flyer* departs Williams, thirty-one miles west of Flagstaff and sixty-five miles south of Canyon Village in Grand Canyon National Park. Amtrak's *Southwest Chief* departs Los Angeles (eastbound) and Chicago (westbound), including intermediate stops at Kansas City, Lamy (Santa Fe), and Albuquerque.

The Titan of Chasms

Set unobtrusively below the rim, Canyon Depot gives little hint of the majesty awaiting your arrival. You are directed to climb the steps behind the depot, proceeding to the stone wall straight ahead. Like the millions before you who were similarly instructed, you arrive on the brink of geological time. After drinking in the canyon and catching your breath, you are ready to notice the rustic elegance of El Tovar. Facing the tracks, it greeted you on your climb up the stairs from Canyon Depot; of course, then the canyon was your priority. Now you see that the opposite side of El Tovar also faces the canyon, although nowhere does it touch the rim. The positioning rather asks that you agree with the railroad not to intrude on the canyon itself. Although a different age might have spared the Grand Canyon any embellishments, this hotel encourages preservation. In 1919, thanks in part to the publicity generated by El Tovar, the "titan of chasms" became a national park.

El Tovar was after all the promotional showpiece of the Santa Fe Railway's park campaign. If you stood here on "the brink of immensity," how could you not want this place to be a national park? It was also the theme of the railroad. Today's highway runs several miles to the east, meeting the tracks only briefly north of Williams. Otherwise the railroad keeps its distance, as if indeed resolute about promoting the Grand Canyon without commercial clutter. Avoiding all untoward distractions, the historical route leads to Grand Canyon across a long plateau broken by several banks

From 1913, the Santa Fe Railway released this stunning chromolithograph by Thomas Moran, *Grand Canyon of Arizona from Hermit Rim Road*, to celebrate the road's completion. Known also as West Rim Drive, much of the original alignment is now a trail. Image exclusive of border (not shown), 26¼ × 35 inches. Author's collection.

of rolling hills. Sweeping views of the San Francisco Peaks crown the distance. If blessed by summer rains, wildflowers bloom brilliantly between the ties, gently bent by the trains gliding overhead.

It is again the difference between the railroad and the highway. The highway constantly directs your attention to everything it wants to sell. The railroad shows you the West. Meanwhile, like the bottom of a wide bowl, the plateau is deepest at its center. The South Rim of Grand Canyon dramatically awaits, but only after the railroad has restored 1,500 feet of elevation. It is a wondrous climb, at first in the open, then the train twists into a deepening forest. Hanging branches veer past the window as yellow cliffs loom overhead. Even now, still far back from the highway, little suggestive of civilization breaks the spell.

The arrival at Canyon Depot similarly recalls the difference between historical grandeur and a tourist trap. One moment the train is wedged between stately pines; the next El Tovar breaks into view, regally positioned on its crest above the station. Nearby, Hopi House and Bright Angel Lodge are added reminders of the railroad's architectural influence.

The best part is never to need a car. In summer, shuttles ply between Canyon Village and Hermits Rest along the spectacular West Rim Drive. Off-season, sponsored tours still are offered. Hikers are especially welcome. The scenic Rim Trail is conveniently accessible from everywhere in Canyon Village. Likewise, Bright Angel Trail is just minutes from several lodges and El Tovar.

The uniqueness of Grand Canyon lies in that enduring celebration of both earth and human time. In its depths, rocks as old as two billion years predate the dawn of life. Along the rim, important cultural resources commemorate the time of our decision. Even Grand Canyon was no match for civilization without allowing people to see the park. The point is that only the railroad kept its promise to build responsibly and creatively. Nor was the railroad interested in distracting visitors still miles outside the park. The landscape approaching the park should be just as magical as everything that lay inside. So endures the legacy of the Grand Canyon Railway, certainly the grandest restoration of its time.

For More Information

Grand Canyon National Park: Write the superintendent, Grand Canyon National Park, P.O. Box 129, Grand Canyon, Arizona 86023. Or call 1-928-638-7888.

Cooperating Association (guidebooks, trail guides, seminars, and other specialized information): Write the Grand Canyon Association, P.O. Box 399, Grand Canyon, Arizona 86023. Or call 1-800-858-2808.

Park Lodging and Guided Tours: South Rim: Write Xanterra Parks & Resorts, P.O. Box 699, Grand Canyon, Arizona 86023. Or call 1-303-297-2757.

Train and Lodging Packages: Williams or South Rim: Call 1-800-THE-TRAIN (1-800-843-8724). Or write Fray Marcos Hotel, Grand Canyon Railway, 235 North Grand Canyon Boulevard, Williams, Arizona 86046.

DENALI NATIONAL PARK AND PRESERVE—ALASKA

Gateway Train(s): **Denali Star** (Alaska Railroad) 1-800-544-0552; **McKinley Explorer** (Holland America Line, Gray Line of Alaska) 1-800-544-2206; **Midnight Sun Express** (Princess Cruises and Tours) 1-800-835-8907.

Service Frequency: Full trains operate daily in season, approximately mid-May to mid-September. Call the Alaska Railroad (1-800-544-0552) for schedules, equipment, and frequencies of operation the remainder of the year.

Arrival: Denali [Mount McKinley] National Park and Preserve is the inspiration for and principal destination of this combined train. Arrival is noon (southbound from Fairbanks) and midafternoon (northbound from Anchorage). Package tours and special itineraries provide for any necessary layovers and accommodations. With few exceptions, the park is off-limits to private cars; regular entry is by bus.

Principal Departure Cities: Trains depart Anchorage and Fairbanks as a single unit operated by the Alaska Railroad. Forward are the engines and *Denali Star* of the Alaska Railroad, followed by the train sets of the *McKinley Explorer* and *Midnight Sun Express*.

The Last Frontier

The moment I noticed the train stretching well past the station, I felt I was back in railroading's golden age. It was early fall in Anchorage, Alaska, where I had come to ride the *McKinley Explorer* north to Denali National Park. The train's classic exterior warmly greeted me like the face of a long-lost friend. Why, this was a streamliner from the 1950s, just like the ones I had known at home. Then the western railroads—and several in the East—had reequipped their passenger fleets with brand-new vista domes. Some, like those of the *McKinley Explorer*, ran the length of the entire car, materially adding to the number of passengers who could enjoy the passing views.

Now, on the Last Frontier, I hoped my train would measure up. In that case, the *McKinley Explorer* would not use gimmicks. Its onboard guides would not be into "staging" Alaska but rather would allow the scenery to speak for itself.

Barely minutes after leaving the station my doubts had been put to rest. The *McKinley Explorer* was indeed authentic. Mountains rose on either horizon, their flanks brilliant in autumn yellow. Suddenly a moose bounded beside the train, and as suddenly ducked off into the nearby underbrush. Wow, did you see that? someone asked. Definitely, this was not an oval in some amusement park or a steam ride through suburbia. Even the guide was still quietly smiling while Alaska did the talking.

When he did speak, it was about preserving wilderness—and the fact that Alaska was one of only four states that had placed a total ban on outdoor advertising. Even I had been unaware of that. No wonder the landscape looked authentic. Only the railroad suggested change, and that but a ribbon laid beside the thundering rivers or dropped over the yawning canyons. I was going somewhere that felt like

Alaska Range by J. Craig Thorpe. Depicted as they appeared in 1994, the combined trains of the Alaska Railroad and Holland America approach Denali National Park and Preserve. Oil on canvas, 24 × 18 inches. Courtesy of the artist.

somewhere—now into the imposing Alaska Range, the landscape still resplendent with natural beauty and ringing with names I had never heard of.

Two other trains bracket the *McKinley Explorer*, each distinctive in its own right. The diesel engines and first train set, the *Denali Star*, are owned by the Alaska Railroad. Immediately behind is the *McKinley Explorer*, and behind that the *Midnight Sun Express*. The latest observation cars, known as ultra domes, are today present on every train. Meanwhile, the combined operations make for the longest train—and probably the most elegant—of its kind anywhere in the United States.

A glimpse of Mount McKinley was all I needed to round out a perfect day. I planned to enter Denali National Park and Preserve the following morning, trekking by bus to Wonder Lake. If at least I might see the mountain, my expectation would be relieved. Suddenly, there it was—Mount McKinley—grandly inviting tomorrow's adventurers along the wilderness road through the heart of the park. As the train pulled into Denali station, I imagined myself a century earlier at Gardiner, Montana, making the cross-platform transfer to a stagecoach about to enter the Yellowstone wilderness. It must have been just like this—the train, the excited voices, and everywhere the bubbling anticipation. The next day, I would be one of only twenty-five thousand people annually who add the 190-mile round-trip to Wonder Lake. I thought again about historic Yellowstone, except that my stagecoach tomorrow morning would be running on diesel or gasoline.

"Outside," as Alaskans call it, wilderness of such proportions—of such sweeping magnificence—is largely a distant memory. In Alaska, wilderness is still here and now, even to gracing the length of the Alaska Railroad. Aboard the *McKinley Explorer*, I felt those qualities of the past return. In bending the wilderness we need never break it. Yet again, a train had proved that a gentler passage is always possible, and indeed, what travel should be all about.

For More Information

Denali National Park: Write the superintendent, Denali National Park and Preserve, P.O. Box 9, Denali Park, Alaska 99755. Or call 1-907-683-2294.

Cooperating Association (guidebooks, trail guides, seminars, and other specialized information): Write Alaska Geographic, 810 East Ninth Avenue, Anchorage, Alaska 99501. Or call 1-866-257-2757.

Park Lodging and Guided Tours: The principal railroad companies operate their own lodges or cooperative facilities just outside the park. Contact Holland America, Princess Tours, and the Alaska Railroad at the numbers listed above. The official park concessionaire is Denali Park Resorts, 241 North C Street, Anchorage, Alaska 99501. Or call 1-800-276-7234.

In the Heart of the Park: The classic wilderness experience is Camp Denali, including nearby North Face Lodge. Write Camp Denali, P.O. Box 67, Denali Park, Alaska 99755. Or call 1-907-683-2290.

KLONDIKE GOLD RUSH NATIONAL HISTORICAL PARK AND WHITE PASS & YUKON ROUTE—SKAGWAY, ALASKA

Ho for the Klondike

Although commemorating the historical events of 1897–1898, the Klondike Gold Rush National Historical Park rivals the spectacular scenery of any of our natural parks. Arriving at Skagway by ship, miners struggled over the imposing Coast Range by way of the Chilkoot Pass and the White Pass to reach the gold fields in the Canadian Yukon. The grandeur of the mountains was the last thing on their minds. Chartered in 1898, the White Pass & Yukon immediately searched out a parallel route over White Pass. By 1900, on completion of the railroad, the accessible gold

In *High Country Inspiration* by J. Craig Thorpe, General Electric diesels lead a summit-bound train past Inspiration Point on the White Pass & Yukon Route, Alaska. A special steam excursion pulled by Baldwin locomotive 73 follows below in Glacier Valley. Oil on canvas, 16 × 27 inches. Courtesy of the White Pass & Yukon Route and permission of the artist.

was already playing out. However, the railroad effectively opened the Yukon, and in 1955 originated containerized shipping. In 1982, the bottom dropped out of the ore market and the 110-mile route was closed. Beginning in 1988, the first twenty miles of the railroad from Skagway to White Pass Summit reopened seasonally, showcasing the mountains to cruise-line passengers. Today, sixty-seven miles have been reopened to Carcross, Yukon Territory. As of 2008, the White Pass & Yukon averaged 430,000 summer visitors, well eclipsing its gold rush days.

To be sure, many consider the White Pass & Yukon the most spectacular railroad in North America. Climbing nearly three thousand feet in twenty miles, it is considered among the great feats of civilization, keeping company with the likes of the Panama Canal, Eiffel Tower, and Statue of Liberty as an International Historic Civil Engineering Landmark. Three miles short of the summit, at Inspiration Point, visitors can look all the way back to Lynn Canal at Skagway. Past the summit, now well above the forest, the landscape thrills passengers as windswept and lunar-like. The final stretch to Carcross, beside Bennett Lake, bears witness to towering peaks on either side.

Managed separately by the National Park Service, Klondike Gold Rush National Historical Park then concentrates on the human drama. Located in the original Skagway depot, the park visitor center is actually one of two. Visitors are then amazed to learn that the other is in Seattle, Washington, 975 miles away. Part of Pioneer Square, the Seattle headquarters commemorates where the miners began their journey after loading themselves down with supplies. Of special interest to railroad visitors, Klondike Gold Rush National Historical Park, Seattle, is just two blocks from King Street Station, Amtrak's principal northwest terminal.

In Alaska, the vast majority of visitors arrive by cruise ship between mid-May and mid-September. A variety of package tours is always available. A final distinguished partner, Parks Canada, further interprets the drama of 1898 at the historic Bennett town site.

For More Information

Klondike Gold Rush National Historical Park: Write the superintendent, Klondike Gold Rush National Historical Park, 319 Second Avenue South, Seattle, Washington 98104, or P.O. Box 517, Skagway, Alaska 99840. In Seattle, call 1-206-220-4240; in Skagway, the number is 1-907-983-2921.

Park Lodging and Guided Tours: Contact the White Pass & Yukon Route at 1-800-343-7373. Or e-mail info@whitepass.net. The mailing address is P.O. Box 435, Skagway, Alaska 99840-0435.

INDIANA DUNES NATIONAL LAKESHORE—PORTER, INDIANA

Gateway Train: **Chicago, South Shore & South Bend Railroad** (Northern Indiana Commuter Transportation District). Tickets may be purchased online at http://www.nictd.com/onlinesales.html. For further information call 1-219-926-5744.

Service Frequency: Daily, including weekends and holidays (subject to change). Eastbound trains depart Chicago at Millennium Station (151 East Randolph Street, southwest corner of Randolph Street and Michigan Avenue); also Van Buren Street (corner of Van Buren Street and Michigan Avenue). Westbound trains begin at South Bend Airport at 4485 Progress Drive. In Chicago, buses and taxis connect with Union Station (210 South Canal Street) and all major Amtrak trains.

Arrival: Four stations provide access to the park—Miller, Ogden Dunes, Dune Park, and Beverly Shores.

Doing the Dunes

Early in the twentieth century, midwestern scientists and civic leaders proposed a national park to save the great sand dunes along the south shore of Lake Michigan. Stephen T. Mather, as director of the National Park Service, enthusiastically noted that the park would be just east of Chicago. One of Chicago's three great interurban railroads, the electrified Chicago, South Shore & South Bend, saw another opportunity—more passengers. Certainly, there would be no park quite like it in the United States. The inland sand dunes of the West were far removed from cities. The proposed "Sand Dunes National Park" would be within an hour of a million people and fully accessible by the South Shore Line.

Although World War I cut short the effort, an Indiana Dunes State Park, opened in 1926, preserved two thousand acres of dunes and marshes, prairie remnants and commingling forests. Immediately the South Shore Line called it an urban oasis. Appealing to both excursionists and commuters, the railroad invited visitors to buy a ticket, bring a picnic basket, and settle aboard its train to "do the dunes." Although swimming became the most popular pastime, the railroad saw other possibilities in promoting the natural history of the dunes. Brochures then seasonally directed visitors to the best trails for hiking and viewing wildlife.

It was a good beginning, preservationists agreed. Still, a larger park was needed. Only a fraction of the dunes had been preserved. Worse yet, industry was trucking away some of the largest dunes for a variety of commercial uses.

The logjam persisted for many years. Finally, the election of President John F. Kennedy in 1960 gave preservationists a ray of hope. A staunch supporter of the Cape

From the late 1920s, this evocative eight-page brochure by the South Shore Railroad alerted Chicagoans to the new Indiana Dunes State Park. *Opposite page*: Page three of the brochure details how readers might enjoy the dunes, including where to find their trains. The remaining pages describe the natural changes in "Duneland" throughout the four seasons of the year. Each 8½ × 5½ inches. Author's collection.

Cod National Seashore, Kennedy's softer terminology—downplaying the word *park*—seemed the perfect compromise for the Indiana Dunes. They could simply be called a national lakeshore, or "a biological crossroads," other supporters added. A park need not be massive, or expensive, or in any way patterned after parks in the West.

The strategy worked. Today, there is no finer example of how to save a landscape by defending the mission of parks close to home. In 1983, two longtime activists, Kay Franklin and Norma Schaeffer, invited me to see for myself. Their policy history, *Duel for the Dunes*, had just been released by the University of Illinois Press. Would I contribute to the park's speaker series at the visitor center in celebration of their book? My interest in railroads certainly suggested how to get me there. After arriving from Seattle at Chicago's Union Station, I should find my way to the South Shore Line. If nothing else, I would get to enjoy America's last great interurban railroad. And I might even fall in love with the dunes.

❖ Indiana Dunes State Park ❖

A LITTLE more than an hour from downtown Chicago lies Duneland—unchanged through the ages—for your enjoyment.

You need not travel thousands of miles to see the strange dune country of Algeria, the great woods of the Canadian North, the Sahara, or Florida's beaches. They are here, in our own Chicago area. Fast South Shore Line service puts them almost at your door.

Indiana Dunes State Park, usually called "The Dunes" or "Duneland," is a 2,000-acre tract of virgin hill and timber country set aside by the State of Indiana as a recreational center for this region. The only charge to visitors is on admission, ten cents a person.

The way to enjoy the Dunes is this: plan for a full day, or a half day at least. Put on your hiking togs, take a camera and a lunch (or have one put up for you at Tremont station) and board a fast South Shore Line limited train at Randolph St., Van Buren St., Roosevelt Road, 53rd St. (Hyde Park), 63rd St. (Woodlawn), or Kensington (115th St.) Illinois Central Suburban station.

After you leave the train at Tremont, plunge into the Dunes, pretend you are a pioneer, and hike and climb and rest to your heart's content. At the end of your day there will be a fast, comfortable South Shore Line train to take you back home. No traffic jams will await you—simply seventy miles an hour in a soft chair with a trained motorman doing the driving. In making your arrangements call the Traffic Department, phone Randolph 8200, 79 West Monroe St., or the Outing and Recreation Bureau, phone Randolph 8200, 72 West Adams St., and ask about the low round trip fares to Tremont.

Each season casts its magic spell over Indiana Dunes State Park. To the left are some of the sand cherry bushes whose brilliance in Spring is a thing to delight the hiker. A contrasting note is given in the picture above, showing one of the early snows of winter festooned on the Duneland trees.

The station at Beverly Shores sealed Kay and Norma's promise that my love affair was foreordained. There was at first this incredible railroad and now this classic station, grand assurance that no one need bring a car. Just step off the train and enter wilderness, at most a short walk away. "Do you like it, Al?" asked Kay and Norma, meeting me on the platform. "Not only did we convince Congress to make this park, we got to keep our railroad!"

I wish that Kay and Norma had lived to see what that means today, and all that their scholarship is still accomplishing. Most significant, the size of the park has nearly doubled, now to fifteen thousand acres. They were just a small part of the effort, they reminded me, all of which began long before they were born. Even so, I am grateful that they became the storytellers of a lifetime dream come true. Thanks now to those many lives, each of us may do the dunes responsibly—gloriously—on the equally fascinating South Shore Line.

For More Information

Indiana Dunes National Lakeshore: Write the superintendent, Indiana Dunes National Lakeshore, 1100 North Mineral Springs Road, Porter, Indiana 46304. Or call 1-219-926-7561, extension 3.

Cooperating Association (guidebooks, trail guides, and other specialized information): Write Eastern National, Great Lakes Regional Office, 42 Ashwood Drive, Suite B, Tiffin, Ohio 44883, or call 1-419-447-0031.

Park Lodging and Guided Tours: No major concessionaires operate inside the park, which essentially, except for camping, is still treated as a day park by most visitors. Currently, the Park Service directs visitors to listings of restaurants and accommodations maintained outside the park. Check the Park Service website at http://www.nps.gov/indu/planyourvisit/lodging.htm.

CUYAHOGA VALLEY NATIONAL PARK— BRECKSVILLE, OHIO

Gateway Train(s): **Lake Shore Limited** and **Capitol Limited** (via Cleveland). Call Amtrak toll-free at 1-800-USA-RAIL (1-800-872-7245). The **Cuyahoga Valley Scenic Railroad** operates year-round inside the park, although dates and service frequencies are variable. Call 1-800-468-4070.

Principal Departure Cities: Westbound sections of the *Lake Shore Limited* depart from New York and Boston, becoming a single train in Albany. The westbound *Capitol Limited* originates in Washington, stopping at Harrisburg and Pittsburgh before proceeding to Cleveland. Both trains end and originate eastbound at Chicago's Union Station, with Amtrak connections from the west and south.

Taming the Crooked River

Designated a national park in 2000 after twenty-six years as a national recreation area, Cuyahoga was never an original railroad park. However, having preserved the railroad that preceded it, no park is more deserving of that term. Known on completion as the Valley Railway, the short line opened in 1880, principally bringing coal to Canton, Akron, and Cleveland. Name changes and new owners followed. Although the railroad's fortunes finally declined in the 1960s, the critical right-of-way was never lost. Rather, with the pending establishment of the national recreation area, park supporters and railroad enthusiasts rallied to the opportunity. The railroad would be perfect for carrying visitors and limiting the use of cars. Full ownership of the tracks and right-of-way passed to the National Park Service

A winter train carries visitors through the heart of Cuyahoga Valley National Park. Photograph by Stian Rice. Courtesy of the National Park Service, Cuyahoga Valley National Park.

in 1985. Operations are leased to the Cuyahoga Valley Scenic Railroad, which is private and nonprofit. Trains are scheduled throughout the year, plying the length of the thirty-three thousand acre park. The route is especially popular with hikers and bicyclists, who may exit and return to the train at several points, either to ride the parallel (and equally historic) Ohio & Erie Canal Towpath Trail or to visit sites within the park.

For More Information

Write or call the superintendent, Cuyahoga Valley National Park, 15610 Vaughn Road, Brecksville, Ohio 44141; 1-330-657-2752.

HARPERS FERRY AND CHESAPEAKE & OHIO CANAL NATIONAL HISTORICAL PARKS—WEST VIRGINIA, VIRGINIA, AND MARYLAND

Worth a Voyage across the Atlantic

As you depart by train from Washington, D.C., the historic C & O Canal is the first reminder that the Potomac River is steeped in history. No route was more pivotal in opening the West. Fifty miles upriver, Thomas Jefferson sensed the coming greatness of the country at Harpers Ferry, marveling at the meeting of the Shenandoah and Potomac Rivers. "In the moment of their junction they rush together against the mountain, rend it asunder, and pass off to the sea," he wrote. "This scene is worth a voyage across the Atlantic." Harpers Ferry indeed proved historic. In 1859, John Brown's raid on the federal armory helped speed the coming of the Civil War. Between 1861 and 1865, the town changed hands eight times.

Great history normally would inspire convenient access, especially so close to the nation's capital. However, as of this writing, MARC commuter trains (Maryland Transit Administration) operate Monday through Friday only, excluding national holidays.

Harpers Ferry, West Virginia by J. Craig Thorpe. Courtesy of Union Tank Car Company, Inc., and permission of the artist.

Amtrak's *Capitol Limited*, with through service to Pittsburgh, Cleveland, and Chicago, operates seven days a week, but frustrates a weekend round-trip to Harpers Ferry if either train is full. Simply, the trip by rail requires patience, although in the spirit of Thomas Jefferson it must be admitted that no more compelling destination exists.

Current train schedules are posted on the web. Contact MARC at http://www .mtamaryland.com/services/marc. Amtrak schedules, under timetables (Capitol Limited), are at http://www.amtrak.com/servlet/ContentServer?pagename=Amtrak/HomePage.

NEW RIVER GORGE NATIONAL RIVER—WEST VIRGINIA

Mountain Road to the West

The conclusion of the Civil War in 1865 allowed the Chesapeake & Ohio Railroad to realize its dream of building west. The route chosen through West Virginia was the spectacular New River Gorge. By the 1930s, the C & O had grown famous for its fine passenger service, colorfully advertised by Chessie, the railroad kitten. Even as passenger trains declined in the 1960s, Chessie and the New River's fame endured.

Amtrak's *Cardinal* emerges from Stretchers Neck Tunnel in West Virginia's New River Gorge. Courtesy and copyright of Gary Hartley.

In 1968, a new initiative for preserving the nation's threatened waterways passed Congress as the Wild and Scenic Rivers Act. At first, rivers paralleled by railroads were considered only "recreational"; finally, common sense prevailed. As exemplified by the New River Gorge, some of the finest scenic rivers in the United States owed their survival to protective railroads. After construction, railroads allowed the beauty of the landscape to return, just as highways kept demanding wider and straighter routes. Railroads also provided disciplined access. Once those qualities had been fully recognized, the New River Gorge National River won authorization in 1978.

Today, the successor to Chessie's trains is Amtrak's *Cardinal*, which makes three stops in the gorge. The only drawback is a limited schedule; both the east- and westbound sections of the *Cardinal* operate just three days a week. It is a daylight trip, however; meanwhile, a full seven-day schedule has been proposed. For trains and parks in the service of nature, there is no finer example than the New River Gorge.

Snaking through the New River Gorge past Grandview Point, the tracks of the former Chesapeake & Ohio Railway (now CSX) are a visible reminder of how railroads respect the landscape. Imagine the railroad as a four-lane highway with the trees removed and the hillsides cut away. Courtesy and permission of Gary Hartley.

For More Information

Write the superintendent, New River Gorge National River, P.O. Box 246, Glen Jean, West Virginia 25846-0246. Or call 1-304-465-0508.

KELSO DEPOT, MOJAVE NATIONAL PRESERVE—CALIFORNIA

Few buildings, that is, few restorations, better represent the National Park Service at its finest. Located in the heart of the Mojave Desert in the shadow of the Kelso Dunes, Kelso Depot has literally been rescued from the elements and gloriously returned to life. As easily, the history of this spectacular building could have ended with its demise. Part of the Los Angeles and Salt Lake Railroad (by the 1920s a major subsidiary of the Union Pacific), Kelso Depot began auspiciously in the days of coal and steam. Linking Utah and California, the Los Angeles and Salt Lake chose a right-of-way southwest through Las Vegas, Nevada, then across the Mojave Desert. The topography proved as challenging as that of any western route. Westbound from Las Vegas on entering California, and beginning at Kelso heading east, loomed the imposing Cima Hill grade. The extra locomotives and crews needed to mount the two thousand foot summit inspired Kelso Depot. Principally intended to house and feed railroad workers, Kelso Depot nonetheless opened in 1924 as if surrounded by a city and not a desert. A railroad station should speak to greatness, Union Pacific reasoned. Besides, there was nothing ordinary about this route. As advertised, it was among the principal main lines to the national parks, nor did every train have a dining car. Park-bound passengers would also find the station a welcome meal stop, including, in 1924, the first on their way to Zion, Bryce, and the North Rim of Grand Canyon, using Union Pacific's new Cedar City branch in Utah. Other through sleeping cars using Salt Lake City and Ogden would just as likely be headed for Yellowstone.

Done in the Spanish Mission Revival style, Kelso Depot was meant to impress travelers in either case. By the 1930s, meal stops had virtually ended, but because trains continued to stop for coal and water passengers had time on the platform to stretch their legs. By then, all would have noticed a major railroad complex. A nearby iron mine added workers and families to the community of two thousand.

In a first major blow to Kelso's survival, the mine, its ore no longer necessary, closed at the end of World War II. Next the railroad made dramatic changes. With the growing adoption of diesel power in the 1950s, the need for Kelso's pusher engines gradually waned. Further, in contrast to the large number of workers needed to fuel and water steam locomotives, diesel engines climbed Cima Hill without the added maintenance. Kelso's shops were closed and their workers transferred. By the

Deep in California's Mojave Desert on the main line of the Union Pacific Railroad, the beautifully restored Kelso Depot now greets visitors to the Mojave National Preserve. Courtesy of the National Park Service, Mojave National Preserve.

end of the 1970s, the community had virtually disappeared—its grand remnant the surviving depot. In 1985, Union Pacific mothballed the building and thought seriously of tearing it down. Building aficionados and environmentalists then intervened. Not only was the beauty of Kelso Depot irreplaceable, any park would be proud to have it. A new national park and the restoration of Kelso Depot as a visitor center was just what environmentalists had in mind.

In 1994, the establishment of the Mojave National Preserve as part of the California Desert Protection Act ensured the survival of Kelso Depot. Guided by Park Service architects and historians, critical studies of the building were soon under way. Despite the usual setbacks and delays, funding for the restoration was approved.

A landscape few could have imagined as a national park in 1924 was suddenly both a natural and historical park. On March 25, 2006, more than seven thousand visitors and dignitaries gathered at Kelso Depot for the unveiling and rededication ceremonies.

The final challenge at Kelso Depot remains the nation's challenge—restoring its passenger trains. Meanwhile, the grandeur of the building calls forth several interpretations, none more important than what it means to have national parks. Without the Mojave National Preserve, the loss to the nation would be immeasurable. Whether by nature or the human hand, beauty of this caliber is not easily replaced.

For Further Information

Write or call the superintendent, Mojave National Preserve, 2701 Barstow Road, Barstow, California 92311; 1-760-252-6108. Directions may be obtained at http://www.nps.gov/moja/planyourvisit/directions.htm. The original lunch counter, called the Beanery, serves light meals during daytime hours. Call for days of operation.

YELLOWSTONE HISTORIC CENTER MUSEUM AND OREGON SHORT LINE TERMINUS HISTORIC DISTRICT— WEST YELLOWSTONE, MONTANA

Breaking the twenty-five-year monopoly of the Northern Pacific Railway, the Oregon Short Line, a subsidiary of the Union Pacific, brought the first revenue passengers from Salt Lake City, Ogden, and Pocatello to West Yellowstone on June 11, 1908. A major terminus then evolved, beginning with the depot in 1909. Designed by Gilbert Stanley Underwood, the great dining lodge completed the railroad's efforts in 1925. After passenger service ended in 1960, the Union Pacific donated eight buildings to the town. All are on the National Register of Historic Places.

Visitors naturally gravitate to the dining lodge and depot, neither of which should be missed. Now a museum, the depot colorfully details the coming of the railroad

The West Yellowstone depot and dining lodge of the Union Pacific Railroad appear in this early postcard view from the railroad's water tower. 3½ × 5½ inches. Author's collection.

and the growth of tourism as a regional industry. New exhibits are constantly being mounted and planned. In season, the dining lodge hosts bluegrass concerts, natural history classes, art exhibits, and public lectures. Across the street, the rustic blends with the modern in what is truly an enjoyable western town. Look for a restored yellow bus, always a favorite with visitors, and another good reason to spend the day.

For More Information

Write the Yellowstone Historic Center Office, P.O. Box 1299, West Yellowstone, Montana 59758. Or call 1-406-646-7461. The West Yellowstone Chamber of Commerce also maintains a web page at http://www.westyellowstonechamber.com.

The National Park Service maintains two other sites of exceptional interest in the development of the American Railroad:

Allegheny Portage Railroad National Historic Site, 110 Federal Park Road, Gallitzen, Pennsylvania 16641. Phone 1-814-886-6100. The completion of an inclined-plane railroad between 1831 and 1834 allowed the first railroad crossing of the Allegheny Mountains, linking Pennsylvania and the West.

Golden Spike National Historic Site, P.O. Box 897, Brigham City, Utah 84302. Phone 1-435-471-2209. Replica locomotives (the Jupiter and 119) reenact the Great Event, the driving of the golden spike marking the completion of the first transcontinental railroad on May 10, 1869.

Private restorations also continue to stabilize railroads with significant value to the national parks. Notable mention would include the **Mount Rainier Scenic Railroad**, P.O. Box 250, Mineral, Washington 98355. Telephone 1-360-492-5588. Foothill portions of the original Tacoma Eastern Railroad provide exceptional views of Mount Rainier National Park. Both steam and diesel trips have been restored.

Visitors to Golden Spike National Historic Site, Utah, enjoy scripted reenactments of the Great Event (May 10, 1869), including the privilege of participating as the principal characters in the ceremony marking the completion of the first transcontinental railroad. Courtesy of the National Park Service, Golden Spike National Historic Site.

Tracks and replica engine house at Allegheny Portage Railroad National Historic Site. Courtesy of the National Park Service, Allegheny Portage Railroad National Historic Site.

... *In all its Glory*

Here—you are riding in the dome of one of the planetarium cars of the Missouri Pacific Railroad's Colorado Eagle.

The mighty Rockies fairly leap from the Colorado plain. Sunrise sets their towering peaks on fire. What a pity to confine this wild majesty to the capsule of a window frame! From the dome you look ahead ... above ... behind. The whole scene is yours in all its glory.

Five of the nation's great railroads will have dome cars this year. They are the world's finest cars, built by Budd, originator of the stainless steel streamliner, and sole builder of all-stainless steel railroad cars—the strongest and safest ever to glide along a glistening rail. The Budd Company, Philadelphia.

Budd

Visit the Chicago Railroad Fair, July 20th thru Labor Day

The conviction that the built environment should complement the natural environment remains the promise and lure of trains. Painting by Leslie Ragan. Original 1948 *Holiday* advertisement, 14 × 11 inches. Author's collection.

⚘ EPILOGUE ⚘

THE FUTURE OF DISCOVERY

It is hard for me to believe that I shall find fair landscapes or sufficient wildness and freedom behind the eastern horizon.

—Henry David Thoreau, 1851

FEW HAVE DISCERNED the singular importance of a national landscape with greater insight than the ecologist Aldo Leopold. "I am glad I shall never be young without wild country to be young in," he wrote in his 1949 classic, *A Sand County Almanac*. "Of what avail are forty freedoms without a blank spot on the map?" Even as the railroads transformed the country, they, too, learned to embrace its magnificent "blank spots." Beauty was a resource like any other. The result was our most enviable linkage between industry and the landscape. Railroad designers and executives, no less than poets, writers, and ecologists, understood intuitively that natural beauty filled an important psychological need. Regardless of how well people came to know the earth, the landscape should always feel inspirational. The essence of travel was the belief that anyone (you) could be seeing everything for the very first time.

"The future lies that way to me," Henry David Thoreau wrote in 1851, describing his own fascination with the West. "The earth seems more unexhausted and richer on that side." Even in settled Massachusetts, he felt drawn on his daily walks "between west and southwest," away from Concord, Walden Pond, and the environs of nearby Boston "toward some particular wood or meadow or deserted pasture or hill in that direction." The attraction, like actual wilderness, was a landscape suggesting that Thoreau had gotten there first. "Eastward I go only by force," he concluded, "but westward I go free."

The ultimate power of the national park idea lay in Thoreau's reasoning that future generations needed to discover the land anew. A commitment to parks was all the more remarkable given the population and its average income at the time. In 1900, only 5,000 people visited Yosemite Valley in a nation of 75 million people. In 1915, three railroads fought over the 51,895 visitors who could afford a trip to Yellowstone, then in a nation of 100 million, most of whom still could not afford it.

Writing as early as 1865, the distinguished landscape architect Frederick Law Olmsted defended the need for patience. Within a century, millions would be visiting Yosemite Valley, and no longer just the rich. "[Those] millions who are hereafter to benefit by the Yosemite Act have the largest interest in it," he wrote, "and the largest interest should be first and most strenuously guarded." Aldo Leopold added a timeless ethic for every generation and every landscape. "Examine each question in terms of what is ethically and esthetically right, as well as what is economically expedient. A thing is right when it tends to preserve the integrity, stability, and beauty of the biotic community. It is wrong when it tends otherwise."

As an industry, railroads came closest to agreeing with Olmsted's call for patience and Leopold's admonition to see right from wrong. There remains the disconnect of our age. Without the railroads—without public transportation—so much of our earlier restraint is gone. We are not like Switzerland, for example, sparing our Alps. Our Rocky Mountains and Sierra Nevada are still making way for wider highways. In Switzerland, heavy trucks are shifting back to railroads. By 2014, all freight traffic crossing the Alps will go by train. Rather than enlarge its highways at the expense of the environment, Switzerland has been tunneling the Alps for decades to provide more and faster trains.

Applied to passengers, Europe's standards are even more remarkable. Instead of one train per day there are thousands. Even the smallest communities get perhaps a dozen. Contrast that with the United States, where, as this book goes to press, more than one hundred midsize cities have lost their airline service. With no passenger trains to step in, in effect the majority of those cities are stranded. If in Europe, those cities might not even notice with so many trains to make up for the planes. The threat to America's communities—and the land—is no longer to have that choice.

In our confidence that progress is linear, we keep ignoring the lessons of the past. Nothing comes without limits; there is no lasting technological "fix." We

West of Georgetown, Colorado, the embankment of Interstate 70 (right) contrasts sharply with the Georgetown Loop Railroad (smoking engine against the trees). After a century, the railroad is barely visible. How long before anyone can say that of the highway? Photograph by the author, September 1, 1978.

would rather gamble in the belief that we know inherently what the planet needs. But do we? Now that the era of wilderness has slipped behind us, is not believing in beauty as we develop landscape the only choice we have?

With railroads we were well on the way to achieving that. We need to ask why we stopped. Our national parks are wonderful, but even they are no longer enough. In the greater challenge—preserving landscape—we at least need something besides the argument that Americans are entitled to have it all.

No, we are not. The only way to believe in landscape is to believe in limits, defending beauty with all our hearts. Only then will we find the humility to know what we can and cannot do. The next time we go in search of beauty we might take the train, again to discover how the continent has blessed us and why its grandeur is who we are.

It can't write.
It can't read.
It doesn't have a degree.
It never went to school.
But after books, it's one of the best teachers of American history.

What is it? A big air-conditioned high-level car on the Santa Fe! An enthralling teacher that really carries you away!

Look: Outside its wide windows the whole exciting story of the Wild West unreels. Live. In color:

The Mississippi. Kansas City . . . where the storied Santa Fe Trail begins and the great plains sweep on to Dodge City.

Now, on the horizon, the Rocky Mountains loom. Over Raton Pass, where pony expresses rode hard, we enter the old Spanish and Indian country. Haciendas. Pueblos. Apaches. (*Geronimo!*)

And so to California—the Spanish missions, the Golden Gate, Hollywood, Disneyland!

Your Discover America trip on Santa Fe is an exciting "lesson" 2,000 miles long. And it's waiting for you now on the Super Chief, El Capitan, The Chief, San Francisco Chief, Texas Chief.

Write Dept. A., Room 333, 80 East Jackson Blvd., Chicago, Ill. 60604 for folders about famous Santa Fe trains or see your nearest ticket agent or travel agent.

HOLIDAY/MAY

45

✷ A NOTE ABOUT ✷ THE SOURCES

N PART INSPIRED by previous editions of this book, writers and historians have broadened their coverage of American railroads to include their relationship with the environment. Conversely, this note will serve to acknowledge my colleagues appearing below, to whose work I owe similar debts. Model studies include John R. Stilgoe, *Metropolitan Corridor: Railroads and the American Scene* (New Haven, CT: Yale University Press, 1983); Susan Danly and Leo Marx, editors, *The Railroad in American Art: Representations of Technological Change* (Cambridge, MA: The MIT Press, 1988), and James E. Vance, Jr., *The North American Railroad: Its Origin, Evolution, and Geography* (Baltimore: The Johns Hopkins University Press, 1995). Michael Frome, "Ten Lovely Train Rides," *Woman's Day* (November 1963): 76–77, 134–136, remains among the few early writings by a noted environmentalist to equate railroads with a sense of place. A philosophical history of railroads and the environment is Alfred Runte, *Allies of the Earth: Railroads and the Soul of Preservation* (Kirksville, MO: Truman State University Press, 2006). A superb sourcebook for all railroad subjects is William D. Middleton, George M. Smerk, and Roberta L. Diehl, *Encyclopedia of North American Railroads* (Bloomington: Indiana University Press, 2007).

For the national parks, the principal primary sources include the annual reports of the superintendents of the individual national parks, published by the Government Printing Office, and Record Group 79 at the National Archives, the records of the National Park Service. The J. Horace McFarland Papers, located at the William Penn Memorial Museum in Harrisburg, Pennsylvania, is the best private collection tracing the alliance between railroads and preservationists.

For the role of the Northern Pacific Railroad in the establishment of Yellowstone National Park, there are two important studies by Aubrey L. Haines: *The Yellowstone Story*, 2 vols. (Yellowstone National Park, WY: Yellowstone Library and Museum Association in cooperation with Colorado Associated University Press, 1977); and *Yellowstone National Park: Its Exploration and Establishment* (Washington: Government Printing Office and National Park Service, 1974). In both, Haines proves the role of Jay Cooke and Company. *Nature's Yellowstone* (Albuquerque: University of New Mexico Press, 1974), by Richard A. Bartlett, and *National Parks: The American Experience*, 4th ed. (Boulder, CO: Taylor Trade Publishing), by Alfred Runte, are other scholarly interpretations of the events of 1869–1872.

Thurman Wilkins (with the help of Caroline Lawson Hinckley), *Thomas Moran: Artist of the Mountains*, 2nd ed. (Norman: University of Oklahoma Press, 1998), focuses on the importance of art in the establishment of Yellowstone National Park and remains a basic source for Moran's relationship with Jay Cooke and A. B. Nettleton. Joni Kinsey, *Thomas Moran and the Surveying of the American West* (Washington: Smithsonian Institution Press, 1992), and Nancy K. Anderson et al., *Thomas Moran* (Washington: National Gallery of Art in association with Yale University Press, 1997), elegantly expand on Moran's life and career, including his commissions with the Northern Pacific and other western railroads. Ronald Fields, *Abby Williams Hill and the Lure of the West* (Tacoma: Washington State Historical Society, 1989), describes in splendid detail how the Northern Pacific and Great Northern railways recruited regional artists to paint the national parks.

A stunning *Wonderland* series of guidebooks, published between 1885 and 1906 by the passenger department of the Northern Pacific Railway, proves the railroad's commitment to Yellowstone and that of its passengers, whose testimonials on the park abound. Suggestive supplementary articles cover agriculture, mining, cities, hunting, and wildlife conservation. *Frederick Billings: A Life* (New York: Oxford University Press, 1991), by Robin W. Winks, credits Billings, as president of the Northern Pacific, with ensuring that its construction across Montana protected the scenery of the Yellowstone River Valley. Similarly, Craig Reese, "The Gardiner Gateway to Yellowstone," *The Mainstreeter* 15 (Spring 1996): 5–21, examines the Northern Pacific's historic branch line between Livingston, Montana, and the park. The other side of the railroad's management personality, as reflected in its manipulation of the Mount Rainier National Park Act to gain lowland timber, is summarized in John Ise's *Our National Park Policy: A Critical History* (Baltimore: The Johns Hopkins Press, 1961). A now superior account of the exchange is Carsten Lien, *Olympic Battleground: The Power Politics of Timber Preservation*, 2nd ed. (Seattle: The Mountaineers Books, 2000). Although Mount Rainier deserved to be a national park, the Northern Pacific's profit was excessive. Lee H. Whittlesey, *Storytelling in*

Yellowstone: Horse and Buggy Tour Guides (Albuquerque: University of New Mexico Press, 2007), returns to the railroad's benevolent side, describing its role and that of other railroads in building the visitor experience off the trains.

For the spread of national park promotion among the western railroads, there are literally countless guidebooks, pamphlets, and advertisements, all published by the companies. Especially important is *Sunset* magazine, initially published between 1898 and 1914 by the passenger department of the Southern Pacific Railroad. Early issues reveal the intensity of the railroad's efforts to promote (and preserve) the High Sierra parks of California. Similarly, *The Grand Canyon of Arizona* (Chicago: Atchison, Topeka & Santa Fe Railway, 1902) is a luxurious volume in the tradition of *Wonderland* and *Sunset*, replete with visitor testimonials. As a secondary source, *The Great Southwest of the Fred Harvey Company and the Santa Fe Railway*, by Marta Weigle and Barbara A. Babcock, editors (Phoenix: The Heard Museum, 1996), adds significantly to our understanding of the railroad's promotional efforts. In part, the book builds on T. C. McLuhan's fine, earlier work, *Dream Tracks: The Railroad and the American Indian, 1890–1930* (New York: Harry N. Abrams, 1985). The title is somewhat misleading. McLuhan focuses critically on the broader subject of railroad promotion, with much on Grand Canyon National Park. Carlos A. Schwantes, *Railroad Signatures across the Pacific Northwest* (Seattle: University of Washington Press, 1993), further interprets railroad promotional efforts in a premier region for national parks. Peter T. Maiken, *Night Trains: The Pullman System in the Golden Years of American Rail Travel* (Chicago: Lakme Press, 1989), meticulously crafts an inventory, arranged by state, of every train that still carried sleeping cars as of March 1952. Noteworthy trains serving the national parks are invariably included in what remains the best overview of the actual service.

For John Muir's impressions of the Southern Pacific Railroad, there is *John Muir and His Legacy: The American Conservation Movement* (Boston: Little, Brown and Company, 1981), by Stephen Fox. A noteworthy supplement is Richard J. Orsi, "'Wilderness Saint' and 'Robber Baron': The Anomalous Partnership of John Muir and the Southern Pacific Company for Preservation of Yosemite National Park," *Pacific Historian* 29 (Summer/Fall 1985): 136–56. Building masterfully on that research, Orsi has written a full-length environmental history of the Southern Pacific Railroad, *Sunset Limited: The Southern Pacific Railroad and the Development of the American West, 1850–1930* (Berkeley: University of California Press, 2005). Also relevant is Alfred Runte, *Yosemite: The Embattled Wilderness* (Lincoln: University of Nebraska Press, 1990). For the role of the Milwaukee Road and its subsidiary the Tacoma Eastern Railroad, there is Arthur D. Martinson, *Wilderness Above the Sound: The Story of Mount Rainier National Park* (Boulder, CO: Roberts Rinehart Publishers, 1994). Similarly, Thornton Waite, *Yellowstone Branch of the*

Union Pacific: Route of the Yellowstone Special (Idaho Falls: Thornton Waite, 1997), and *Yellowstone by Train: A History of Rail Travel to America's First National Park* (Missoula, MT: Pictorial Histories Publishing Co., Inc., 2006), detail the efforts of the Union Pacific Railroad (and others) to compete with the Northern Pacific for Yellowstone passengers. Relevant histories of the Yosemite Valley Railroad are Hank Johnston, *Railroads of the Yosemite Valley* (Long Beach, CA: Johnston-Howe Publications, 1963), and Jack A. Burgess, *Trains to Yosemite* (Berkeley, CA: Signature Press, 2005). The Yosemite National Park Research Library also contains records and photographs of the company.

Two contemporary publications describe Louis W. Hill and the Great Northern Railway's development of Glacier National Park: Mary Roberts Rinehart, "Through Glacier National Park with Howard Eaton," parts I and II, *Collier's* 57 (April 22 and 29, 1916), and Rufus Steele, "The Son Who Showed His Father: The Story of How Jim Hill's Boy Louis Put a Ladder to the Roof of His Country," *Sunset* 34 (March 1915): 473–85. C. W. Guthrie, *All Aboard for Glacier: The Great Northern Railway and Glacier National Park* (Helena, MT: Farcountry Press, 2004), provides a modern history of the relationship between the railroad and the park. The proceedings of the national parks conferences of 1911, 1912, 1915, and 1917, published by the Government Printing Office for the U.S. Department of the Interior, coupled with the hearings on the National Park Service bill before the House Committee on Public Lands, disclose unequivocally how much the railroads wanted to serve and improve the national parks. The History E-Library of the National Park Service at http://www .nps.gov/history/history/ is a magnificent source for continuing research, containing thousands of publications in the public domain, including park histories, original park brochures, and the agency's distinguished Handbooks and Publications series.

For the relationship between the railroads and Stephen T. Mather during his tenure as director of the National Park Service, there remains Robert Shankland, *Steve Mather of the National Parks*, 3rd ed. (New York: Alfred A. Knopf, 1970); Donald C. Swain, *Wilderness Defender: Horace M. Albright and Conservation* (Chicago: University of Chicago Press, 1970); Horace M. Albright as told to Robert Cahn, *The Birth of the National Park Service: The Founding Years, 1913–33* (Salt Lake City: Howe Brothers, 1985); and Horace M. Albright and Marian Albright Schenck, *Creating the National Park Service: The Missing Years* (Norman: University of Oklahoma Press, 1999). These books of course focus on Mather and Albright, leaving the impression that the railroads were following them. A more balanced perspective is Robin W. Winks, "The National Park Service Act of 1916: 'A Contradictory Mandate'?" *Denver University Law Review* 74 (1997): 575–623. The railroads were hardly bit players, Winks confirms, Mather and Albright's singular contributions notwithstanding.

In recent years, the role of the railroads in building and/or contributing to park infrastructure has finally received the attention it also deserves. Ray Djuff and Chris Morrison, *View with a Room: Glacier's Historic Hotels and Chalets* (Helena, MT: Farcountry Press, 2001), is a model history focusing on a single park. Christine Barnes, in *Great Lodges of the National Parks*, volume 1 (Bend, OR: W. W. West, Inc., 2002), and volume 2 (Portland, OR: Graphic Arts Books, 2008), writes definitively on all of the original railroad parks. Ruth Quinn, *Weaver of Dreams: The Life and Architecture of Robert C. Reamer* (Yellowstone National Park, WY: Leslie and Ruth Quinn Publishing, 2004), is a biography of Yellowstone's premier architect and his years under commission to the Northern Pacific Railway. Reamer's distinguished contemporary in the American Southwest, Mary Elizabeth Jane Colter, is further the subject of Virginia Grattan, *Mary Colter: Builder Upon the Red Earth* (Grand Canyon, AZ: Grand Canyon Association, 1992), and Arnold Berke and Alexander Vertikoff, *Mary Colter: Architect of the Southwest* (Princeton, NJ: Princeton Architectural Press, 2001).

Overviews of railroad advertising as an inducement for environmental preservation may be found in special issues of *California History* 70 (Spring 1991) and *Journal of the West* 31 (January 1992). Kirby Lambert, "The Lure of the Parks," *Montana: The Magazine of Western History* 46 (Spring 1996): 42–55, skillfully augments my interpretations, including examples of previously unpublished railroad art. A new journal of the Colorado Plateau, *Sojourns*, includes my overview of railroads and landscape, "Every Magic Mile: Railroads and Renewal" (volume 1, winter/spring 2006): 22–31. An intriguing book by James Howard Kunstler hints at the price of losing railroads, *The Geography of Nowhere: The Rise and Decline of America's Man-Made Landscape* (New York: Simon and Schuster, 1993). The man-made landscape has obviously worsened, as famously symbolized in 1963 by the loss of New York City's Pennsylvania Station. It was undoubtedly the demolition crime of the twentieth century. An illustrated, historical remembrance is Lorraine B. Diehl, *The Late, Great Pennsylvania Station* (New York: American Heritage, 1985). The price of railroad abandonment is further the subject of two books by Joseph P. Schwieterman, *When the Railroad Leaves Town: American Communities in the Age of Rail Line Abandonment—Eastern United States* (Kirksville, MO: Truman State University Press, 2001); and *When the Railroad Leaves Town: American Communities in the Age of Rail Line Abandonment—Western United States* (Kirksville, MO: Truman State University Press, 2004).

Resuming a positive tone, the possibility of restoring railroads, the above-mentioned *Journal of the West* (January 1992) contains excellent articles by Al Richmond and Gordon Chappell—Richmond's on the rebuilding of the Grand Canyon Railway, "Renaissance: Breathing New Life into a Legendary Railway," pp. 60–68, and

Chappell's on the early development of what was to become Death Valley National Monument, "By Rail to the Rim of Death Valley: Construction of the Death Valley Railroad," pp. 10–19. Readers will also wish to consult Al Richmond's *Cowboys, Miners, Presidents, and Kings: The Story of the Grand Canyon Railway* (multiple editions, 1989–present), and *Rails to the Rim: Milepost Guide to the Grand Canyon Railway* (1990), both published in Flagstaff, Arizona, by the Grand Canyon Railway. *A Vision for Grand Canyon National Park* (Flagstaff, AZ: Grand Canyon Railway, 1997) is an imaginative look at Grand Canyon were the park—European-style—to include a light-rail system. Meanwhile, Gordon Chappell et al., *Kelso Depot Historic Structure Report, Mojave National Preserve, California* (Washington: United States Department of the Interior, National Park Service, January 1998) speaks to a model restoration at a Park Service site, inviting our imagination about the future.

Indeed, where do we go from here? John Stilgoe's *Train Time: Railroads and the Imminent Reshaping of the United States Landscape* (Charlottesville: University of Virginia Press, 2007) suggests that America's railroad renaissance may already have begun. James McCommons, *Waiting on a Train: The Embattled Future of Passenger Rail Service—A Year Spent Riding across America* (White River Junction, VT: Chelsea Green Publishing, 2009), takes a more cautious view. My own "Trains for Parks: A Second Chance," *National Parks* 68 (March/April 1994): 30–34, similarly addresses the steps that would be necessary to reshape the nation's thinking. Kay Franklin and Norma Schaeffer, *Duel for the Dunes: Land Use Conflict on the Shores of Lake Michigan* (Urbana: University of Illinois Press, 1983), proves again the importance of keeping railroads viable. Our landscapes need never lose their beauty to development so long as we dare to know what beauty is.

✄ INDEX ✄

❧ ABOUT THE AUTHOR ❧

AN INTERNATIONALLY recognized expert on national parks and railroads, Alfred Runte is based in Seattle, Washington. He was recently an adviser to the Ken Burns PBS documentary *The National Parks: America's Best Idea* and appeared in all six episodes of the Emmy Award–winning series. Runte has also been a guest on *Nightline*, *The Today Show*, *48 Hours*, the History and Travel channels, and speaks frequently in public forums on the need to protect our parks. His other books include *Allies of the Earth: Railroads and the Soul of Preservation*, *Yosemite: The Embattled Wilderness*, and the fourth edition of his critically acclaimed *National Parks: The American Experience*. In April 2011, Runte was elected to membership in the College of Arts and Sciences Hall of Fame at Illinois State University (his master's degree institution) "in recognition of exemplary achievement" as a teacher and public scholar.